Scats
and
Tracks
of the
Southeast

A Field Guide to the Signs of Seventy Wildlife Species

James C. Halfpenny, Ph.D., and Jim Bruchac

Illustrated by Todd Telander

FALCON®

GUILFORD, CONNECTICUT
AN IMPRINT OF THE GLOBE PEQUOT PRESS

_A_FALCONGUIDE®

Copyright © 2002 by The Globe Pequot Press

Falcon and FalconGuide are registered trademarks of The Globe Pequot Press.

Cover photo © Jack Hoehn

Library of Congress Cataloging-in-Publication Data
Halfpenny, James C.
    Scats and tracks of the Southeast: a field guide to the signs of seventy wildlife species / James C. Halfpenny and Jim Bruchac; illustrated by Todd Telander.— 1st ed
    p. cm.— (Scats and tracks series)
ISBN 0–7627–1140–X
1. Animal tracks—Southern States. I. Bruchac, Jim. II. Title. III. Series.
QL768 .H358 2001
591.975—dc21   2001040713

♻ Text pages printed on recycled paper

Manufactured in the United States of America
First Edition/First Printing

To Diann, my alpha partner, ursophile, and tracking friend, for all her loving support and help.

JH

In memory of my grandfather, Joseph Bruchac, Jr., whose feet followed these tracks long before I was born.

JB

Contents

Acknowledgments

First and foremost, I wish to thank all my students for their years of questions and help, but most of all for the time we've shared tracking and studying in the field. I also wish to thank Steve Engel (Animal Tracks, Bend, OR) for providing information on nutria tracks, Terry McEneany (Yellowstone National Park) for his help with bird tracks, and Phil Tanimoto for his help with ocelot tracks.

JH

I would like to thank all those that helped with my research including Mike R. Pelton, Ph. D., Frank T. Varmarer (bear weights and distribution), Eric Andrews, George Bumann (species distribution), Rob DiGiovanni (Senior Biologist, River Head Foundation for Marine Research), and especially my wife, Jean Bruchac.

JB

Introduction

In the late 1970s, the era of watchable wildlife arrived in the United States. Baby boomers wanted to turn to and experience the outdoors. Television brought wildlife closer than ever. Bird-watching thrived. Now more than ever, millions of people want to watch wild animals. Wildlife are not always easy to find and observe, though. Finding their tracks and signs is an exciting alternative to actually seeing the animals. Trackable wildlife adds another dimension to the outdoor experience. Todd, Jim, and I wish to share that dimension, the joy of reading stories written in the soil and snow.

Upward of ten books on tracking have been written in the United States during each decade of the twentieth century. Most are general, covering the United States or all of North America. In *Scats and Tracks of the Southeast*, we focus on one biogeographic region, with details about the region's most common or characteristic species of mammals, birds, reptiles, and amphibians. (We have included a few rare species because of their particular interest or significance in a region. For example, what a coup it would be to document an ocelot in Texas or a mountain lion in Georgia.) We've intentionally limited the number of species covered in order to keep the information manageable. This guide is small, allowing you to carry it in a pack or pocket and use it frequently.

As your knowledge and interest in tracking grows, you may want to find additional information and help. Key references are listed in Selected Reading. For a more detailed investigation of tracking, I recommend my book *A Field Guide to Mammal Tracking in North America* (1986, Johnson Publishing, Boulder, Colorado) and titles by Olaus Murie, L. R. Forrest, and Paul Rezendes.

Two organizations will, in computer parlance, provide interactive access to expand your tracking background. A Naturalist's World (ANW) is an ecologically oriented company dedicated to providing educational programs and materials reflecting the natural history of North America. Diann Thompson and I run the daily business, teach classes, and lead programs. Our on-site classes provide hands-on experience and in-depth information about animals, their tracks, and the ecology of their environments. In addition to tracking classes, our field programs cover bears, wolves, winter ecology, the northern lights, and alpine ecology. ANW also provides books, videos, slides shows, and computer programs for self-study and as teaching and field aids. You can check out ANW on the Internet at www.tracknature.com. Class schedules, product information, and information about ANW can be obtained from P.O. Box 989, Gardiner, MT 59030, phone (406) 848–9458, or on the Web at www.tracknature.com.

The Ndakinna Wilderness Project—run by Jim Bruchac—offers animal tracking classes and adventures for all ages. Tracking trips venture into the Adirondacks and other Northeastern forests by foot, snowshoe, or sea kayak. Other topics offered by Ndakinna include natural history, basic wilderness skills, and northeastern native culture. Many classes take place at the Ndakinna Education Center & Nature Preserve, run by Jim and his wife, Jean, in Greenfield Center, New York. Class schedules and general information can be obtained from 23 Middle Grove Road, Greenfield Center, NY 12833, phone (518) 583–9980, or on the Web at www.ndakinna.com.

Keep on tracking!

—*James C. Halfpenny*

About tracking

Tracking is for everyone—beginner and expert, young and old. The fun of nature's challenge is solving the mystery written in the trail. Prepare yourself by learning the background and basics of tracking before exercising your skills in the field.

Field notes and preserving tracks

To the natural history detective, the track and trail are things of great beauty and significance. They tell part of the story of an animal's life. Tracks and trails deserve to be preserved, both to increase your knowledge and as a record you can share with others. Preservation is commonly made in the form of written notes, casts, or photographs.

Perhaps the most important item in the naturalist's tool kit is the field notebook. Field notes can jog the memory and facilitate better retention of knowledge. The notes can be analyzed later and can be preserved as records of chance encounters. Writing good field notes is an art form and a science in itself. Field notes are a source of pride when shown to others and may gain recognition for recording rare and unusual events. And need we mention how quickly memories, especially for details, fade when not preserved?

While great and complex systems have been designed for complete and accurate records, there are really but three requirements for the tracker: ruler, paper, and pen. With these, every trail becomes a record for later analysis and sharing. We cannot emphasize enough the importance of enhancing your tracking experience by keeping notes to which you can later refer!

A simple 3-by-5-inch notebook and a 6-inch ruler are adequate to get started. Use a pencil or a pen that won't run if your notes get wet. To facilitate taking notes, A Naturalist's World offers a waterproof notebook that contains information about footprint groups, gaits, and how to track; data sheets for recording information; and English and metric rulers imprinted on the back cover. See the Introduction for contact information for A Naturalist's World.

Tracks may also be preserved by photographing and making casts. Good photographs can be made by any modern camera that can take a good close-up. When taking pictures, try to fill the viewfinder with the footprint. Get as close as possible. Always include a ruler or some object in the photo to provide a sense of scale. Avoid using hats, gloves, hands, or objects without a straight edge; round edges do not lend themselves to making accurate measurements from a photo. Also, step back and take photographs of the trail to show the footprints that we photographed close-up. Fast films (ASA of 200 or higher) are generally best, because tracks are often found in dark places, especially ground surfaces.

Plaster casts are the old standby for preserving tracks. We suggest a casting kit that includes a one-gallon (four-liter) plastic jar with a screw lid for carrying dry plaster, a narrow spatula, a plastic mixing cup such as those sold for medium-sized drinks, paper for wrapping and transporting the finished cast, and a plastic sack for cleanup. A bottle of water may be needed if water is not available on site. Two pounds of plaster will make at least four coyote-sized track casts.

Purchase plaster from a lumberyard or hardware store, as prices will be more reasonable than at a drugstore or hobby shop. Almost any plaster will work, including plaster of paris, hydrocal, ultracal, or hydrostone. Avoid getting plaster for wallboard or patching compound, however.

These plasters are formulated to be slightly flexible on walls and do not get hard enough for casts.

Two factors are critical to preventing casts from breaking: thickness and density. In the field, thickness is assured by building a wall around the track to contain the plaster. Natural objects such as twigs, stone, and dirt may be used to make a retaining wall 0.25 to 0.5 inch (0.6 to 1.3 cm) above the track. Alternatively, walls in the form of plastic strips cut from milk cartons or other plastic containers may be taken to the field. Proper density is assured by mixing two parts of plaster to one part of water by volume (read instructions on plaster container) to create a mixture similar in consistency to thick pancake batter or a milk shake.

Place your spatula close to the track and pour onto the spatula to break the fall of the plaster into the footprint. Working quickly so that the plaster does not set and become too thick, gently pour the plaster first into the fine detailed areas of the footprint and then the rest of the print. Finally, pour the plaster to an appropriate depth (inside the retaining wall) to keep the cast from breaking. Vibrating the spatula up and down across the top of the plaster will cause it to settle evenly and create a smooth back for the cast. Allow the plaster to dry for thirty minutes, or as long as recommended on the plaster package. Gently pick the plaster up by digging your fingers under opposite sides of the cast, and turn the cast over onto one hand. Now wash off the dirt by rubbing the cast with your fingertips under the flowing water of a stream or a hose. Do not wash the cast in a sink, as the plaster may clog the drain. Let the cast continue to cure for several days in a warm, dry environment. If you need to transport it, wrap the cast in paper. Never wrap the cast in plastic; trapped moisture can cause it to crumble.

While special techniques are needed for dust and snow, this procedure will allow casting in many situations.

Remember, carry a plastic garbage bag and always clean up your mess. No sign of your plaster should remain to reduce the experience of others who happen by later.

Scats and bird pellets

Scats and bird pellets (also called cough pellets or castings) are often helpful for identifying an animal or completing the story written in the trail. Scats and pellets help identify not only what the animal was eating, but who the animal was. However, it should be noted that scats and pellets won't help you identify an animal with as much certainty as tracks will. Many animals make similar scats and pellets that are difficult to tell apart.

The scats of many carnivores are very similar, especially when the diet is mostly meat. Size alone does not provide a definitive answer because of the wide range of diameters produced within a species and even by a single member of a species. For example, fox produce scats ranging in size from 0.3 to 0.8 inch (0.8 to 2.0 cm), coyotes produce scats from 0.5 to 1.3 inches (1.3 to 3.3 cm), and wolves produce scats from 0.5 to 1.5 inches (1.3 to 3.8 cm), and we all know how our own scat varies in size and shape. When judging size, consider both the total quantity of scat and the size of individual pieces. Moist food produces slimmer scats, while fibrous diets produce wider scats.

Given these cautions, scat shapes can be used to identify general groups of animals (see page xviii). Spherical shapes flattened top to bottom are deposited by members of the rabbit order. Elongate spheres are deposited by rodents and shrews, and larger sizes by deer and their relatives. Long, thick cords are deposited by dogs, bears, and raccoons. Dog scats typically have tapered ends, while those from bears and raccoons are blunt. Cats also produce thick cords with blunt ends, but they tend to be constricted or even broken into short segments. Cords that loop back on themselves are produced by members of the weasel family. Birds, in general, produce long, thin cords or shapeless, semiliquid excretions. Reptiles and amphibians may produce small elongate spheres or long, thin cords. White, nitrogenous urine deposits, found only on the scats of birds, reptiles, and amphibians, separate them from mammal scats. Scats may be confused with cough pellets. Many bird groups, including owls, raptors, crows, ravens, jays, magpies, gulls, herons, storks, flycatchers, and kingfishers, produce cough pellets in addition to scats. Birds pass digestive juices through what they have eaten to remove the nutrients. Hair, bones, beaks, claws, and other nondigestible parts accumulate in the gizzard (anterior portion of stomach), are compressed, and are coughed up as pellets. Food remnants in the pellet are easy to identify and tell much about the bird's feeding habits and even the habitats it frequents.

Pellets are grayish in color and are spherical or long and tapered at both ends. When fresh, they are covered by mucus and appear dark black. Pellets are found mainly at roosting sites and nests, and occasionally at

cough pellet

feeding areas. They are deposited singly, but many may accumulate beneath a tree where a bird is roosting, nesting, or perching. Nitrogenous scat deposits on the ground or twigs may help verify an object as a pellet.

The diameter of the throat determines the maximum diameter of the pellet. In general, large birds produce larger pellets. Shape and diameter allow one to distinguish to some degree among species. Birds generally produce two pellets per day and regurgitate just before taking flight. The time of day when feeding occurred may affect the sample of food items. For example, owls tend to

Shapes of scats

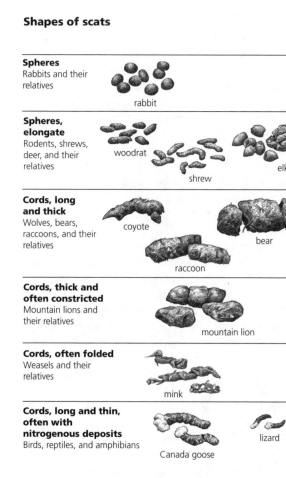

Spheres
Rabbits and their
relatives

rabbit

**Spheres,
elongate**
Rodents, shrews,
deer, and their
relatives

woodrat

shrew

elk

**Cords, long
and thick**
Wolves, bears,
raccoons, and their
relatives

coyote

bear

raccoon

**Cords, thick and
often constricted**
Mountain lions and
their relatives

mountain lion

Cords, often folded
Weasels and their
relatives

mink

**Cords, long and thin,
often with
nitrogenous deposits**
Birds, reptiles, and amphibians

Canada goose

lizard

feed on mammals that come out only at night, while hawks feed on animals that are out during the daylight hours.

Anatomy and footprint nomenclature

The feet of mammals, birds, reptiles, and amphibians are anatomically complex, and that complexity shows in their footprints. Knowing something of the anatomy of their feet will aid in footprint identification and interpreting trails.

The toes of all animals are numbered from the inside of the foot out (the inside of the foot being the side closest to the animal). Therefore, in humans and other mammals, the thumb or big toe (if present) is number 1 and the little finger or little toe is number 5. In birds, toe 1 (if present) points backward. Over evolutionary time, toes of animals have become reduced in size or have disappeared altogether. In cats and dogs, toe 1 is absent or reduced to a small toe called a dewclaw. In deer, elk, sheep, and similar mammals, toe 1 is absent and toes 2 and 5 are reduced and form dewclaws. Toes 3 and 4, the clouts, form the cloven hoof. In pronghorn antelope, toes 1, 2, and 5 are absent. In birds, toe 5 is absent, and toe 1 is often reduced and occasionally is absent. In the amphibians covered here, toe 1 has been lost from the front foot.

Track measurements

To more accurately determine the animal's foot size from its tracks, mountain lion researchers Fjelline and Mansfield (1989) developed the minimum outline method of measuring tracks.

Place your hand on a hard surface, a table for instance. Note the contact area of your hand with that surface. If your hand went no deeper into that surface, your handprint would have only one size: the minimum outline. If your hand were to sink deeper into the surface—as it would if the surface were, say, mud—it would create a series of variable outlines, each larger than the one before, as the mud flowed around the curved surface of your hand. All footprints have a minimum outline, but only prints that sink into a surface have variable outlines.

Note that while the variable outline of a footprint may only be several millimeters wider than the minimum outline, those few millimeters have a large visual effect. The human eye sees area, and area increases with the square of a linear measurement. In short, a few millimeters of width adds a lot of area to a footprint.

The minimum outline size does not change for different surfaces and therefore provides a standard for comparison among surfaces. And though one animal may leave many sizes of footprints depending on surface, slope, and speed, there is only one minimum outline for every footprint an animal might leave. The minimum outline measurement is the only constant and consistent size in tracking.

To measure the minimum outline, study the bottom of a print. The *break point* where the rounded pad turns upward is the edge of the minimum outline. Use this edge to measure tracks.

Assigning the break point is a subjective judgment and no two people will always mark it at exactly the same

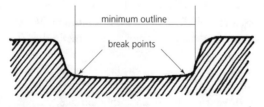

cross section of footprint in ground

point. However, testing has shown that an individual tracker using the minimum outline method can reduce personal variation in measurement and that groups of trackers using this method will also become more consistent in their measurement of tracks. Remember the computer rule GIGO: Garbage in, garbage out. You cannot get quality measurements from a bad track. Quality measurements are the tracker's goal, and using minimum outline methods greatly reduces over-exaggeration and variance in measurement.

All measurements in this guide are minimum outline measurements.

The measurements in *Scats and Tracks of the Southeast* are mostly averages gathered from years of tracking. Averages include only animals judged to be adult. However, it is important to remember the great size variation among animals. Every animal was small once in its life, and some never get big. Males are often substantially larger than females. Regional variations in mammal sizes also occur. For example, coyotes are smaller in the southwestern United States and larger in the northeastern part of the country. Their tracks vary accordingly. Therefore, a track in the field may be considerably larger or smaller than the measurements provided. Use track measurements only as a rough guideline, not an absolute rule.

Gaits and trails

Coordinated muscle movements result in the various gaits used by animals. In the simplest form, when moving on two legs (bipedal movement) an organism can *walk*, *run*, and *hop*. When moving on four legs (quadrupedal movement) an organism can *walk*, *trot*, *lope*, *gallop*, *bound*, and *pronk* (also called *stot*). Though other gaits exist, we will confine our discussion to these basic gaits. Each gait leaves a characteristic pattern that may be modified by changes in speed and body angle. The combination of footprints is called the *trail*. The bipedal walk and run and the quadrupedal walk and trot result in gaits that are *symmetrical*. The right side of the trail is a mirror image of the left side. The trail patterns for these gaits are the same, alternating right-left pattern, and they differ only by the stride being longer in the run and trot than it is in the walk. In the run and trot, the straddle, the distance from the right edge of the rightmost pad (see pages xxvi and xxx) to the left edge of the leftmost pad, also tends to be narrower than it is in the walk.

Quadrupedal movement also results in gaits that are *asymmetrical* (the right half of the trail is not always a mirror image of the left), including lope, gallop, bound, hop, and pronk. These gaits produce patterns that include all four footprints (two fronts, two hinds, two rights, and two lefts) in a group separated from the next group by a space where no footprints appear.

In *gallops*, the feet, front and rear, that move first (or *lead*) will determine whether the gallop will form a Z-shaped or C-shaped pattern. When the front and hind feet on the same side lead, the pattern takes on a Z shape, called a *transverse* gallop. A right-front lead with a left-hind lead or vice versa results in a C-shaped pattern, called a *rotatory* gallop. Thus, there are four possible gallop patterns.

Bounds (also known as hops and jumps) are characterized by the synchronization of the hind feet; both

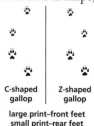

C-shaped gallop | Z-shaped gallop

large print–front feet
small print–rear feet

strike the ground at the same time, side by side. The front feet strike the ground at a different time than the hind feet. In a full bound, the front feet are synchronized and strike the ground side by side at the same time. In a half bound, only the hind feet are synchronized and the front feet hit the ground staggered. Animals that mostly use full bounds, also called hops, live in trees (tree squirrels and songbirds), whereas those that mostly use half bounds live on the ground (ground squirrels and rabbits).

In a *pronk* (also called a *stot*), all four feet strike the ground at the same time, with the front feet side by side and forward of the hind feet, which are also side by side. This gait is often used by deer to gain height and increase time in the air to look around.

To increase peripheral vision, non-primate mammals have eyes placed toward the side of their heads, not flat on their face like humans. By turning sideways, a prey species can see what is pursuing it and where it needs to go to escape. The predator, by turning sideways, can see what it is chasing and where the rest of the predator pack is.

Consequently, quadrupedal mammals have evolved to use all gaits while their body is turned to the side. These *side gaits* result when the animal's heavy head deviates from the line of travel and the body turns sideways. First, the front feet respond by moving toward the side of the trail where the head is. Then, as the head turns more, the hind feet move to the side away

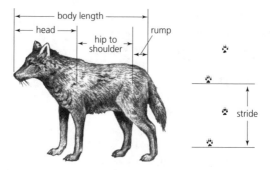

estimating mammal length from stride

from the head. The greater the head movement, the greater the angle of the side gait. Common examples are the side trot and side gallop often used by canids. These are often called a dog trot or dog gallop.

An animal's size is also reflected in its gait patterns. When a mammal is walking with its normal gait, for example, the stride is 1.1 to 1.25 times longer than the distance from the hip to the shoulder joint. Using this crude relationship, body size can be judged from a walking stride. A 22-inch stride indicates a hip-to-shoulder length of 20 inches. Add to the hip-to-shoulder distance an estimate for the head length beyond the shoulder joint and an estimate of the rump length beyond the hip joint to get a total estimate of animal body length.

Speed also modifies gait patterns in trails. There are three rules governing how pattern changes as speed changes:

1. As speed increases, the hind foot lands farther forward than the front footprint on the same side. Conversely, as speed decreases, the hind foot lands farther back in relation to the front footprint.
2. As speed increases, stride increases.
3. As speed increases, straddle usually decreases.

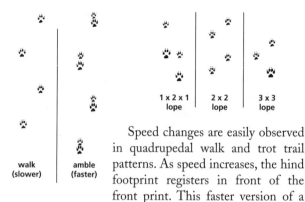

walk
(slower)

amble
(faster)

1 x 2 x 1
lope

2 x 2
lope

3 x 3
lope

Speed changes are easily observed in quadrupedal walk and trot trail patterns. As speed increases, the hind footprint registers in front of the front print. This faster version of a walk is called an amble. The faster version of a trot doesn't have a name. When the animal slows to the point that the hind feet are registering behind the front prints, the animal may be stalking something. Trots are separated from walks by having a stride two or more times greater than the estimated hip-to-shoulder distance of an animal. A slow version of the gallop is also recognizable. When a gallop slows to the point that one or more hind feet register behind the leading edge of the frontmost footprint in a group pattern, the gait is called a *lope*. The gait is still a gallop, it's just a slow gallop.

Trail measurements

The terms *stride*, *group*, *intergroup*, and *straddle* describe the size of an animal trail. The stride is measured from the point where a foot touches the ground surface to where the same point of the same foot next touches the surface, and consists of one group and one intergroup measurement. The *group* consists of all four footprints (two fronts, two hinds, two lefts, two rights), while the *intergroup* is the distance between groups. Gait patterns take their name from the configuration of the group. The stride provides an indication of size in a walking animal and an indication of relative speed for other gaits (see pages xxii and xxiii).

The *straddle* indicates the width of the trail and is measured from the outside rightmost pad of the outside right footprint of a group to the outside leftmost pad footprint of the same group. The outside edges of the trail are used because the inside of footprints overlap for many carnivore species.

Stride, group, and intergroup are all measured parallel to the trail, while the straddle is measured at right angles to the trail. Select a straight section of trail on level ground to measure. The slightest curve in the trail will distort the straddle measurement.

Glossary of terms

amble: a fast walk in which the hind footprint registers anterior to the front footprint. See illustration on page xxv.

asymmetrical: not symmetrical; that is, one side is not a mirror image of the opposite side.

bound: a gait in which both hind feet strike the ground at the same time, side by side. If the front feet also land side by side, the motion is said to be a *full bound*. A *half-bound* occurs when one foot strikes the ground in front of the other. See illustration on page xxiii.

clout: term used to refer to toe 3 or toe 4 of the hoof. See illustration on page xxxi.

convergent toes: toes 2 and 4 of ducks, geese, and swans, which bend toward the foot axis, especially at the tips. Compare to *divergent* toes.

cord: See scat shape.

cough pellet: remnants of bones and hair coughed up by many bird species after feeding on prey.

dewclaw: toe that over evolutionary time has become reduced in size and raised on the leg, away from the other toes; for example, toe 1 in dogs and toes 2 and 5 in deer.

diagnostic: providing certain identification of an animal or its sign.

digitigrade: walking on the tips of the toes. Dogs and cats, for example, are digitigrade. Tracks left by digitigrade animals rarely show a sole. Compare to *plantigrade*.

digit: one of the toes of an animal.

digital pad: See *pad*.

distal webbing: See *webbing*.

divergent toes: Toes that are straight or turn out from the *foot axis* at the tips, specifically toes 2 and 4 of sea gulls. Compare to *convergent* toes.

foot axis: imaginary line down the center of the foot. It runs between toes 3 and 4 in deer and their relatives, and down toe 3 of other mammals. In birds, the foot axis also runs down toe 3.

fringe: webbing attached to a single toe. May have a smooth edge, known as a *simple fringe* or *simple lobe*, or it may be wavy, in which case it is said to have *indented lobes*.

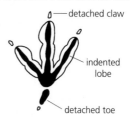

detached claw

indented lobe

detached toe

full bound: See *bound*.

gait: term for the type(s) of movement an animal uses when moving. Examples of gaits include *walk*, *amble*, *trot*, *bound*, and *gallop*. Gaits are defined by the mechanics of body movement, not by speed.

gallop: a gait in which hind feet move around the front feet and (usually) strike the ground in front of the front feet. Galloping forms distinct group patterns (two fronts, two hinds, two lefts, two rights) separated by an intergroup distance from the nest set of four feet. Gallops fall into two basic patterns: Z-shaped and C-shaped.

group: a subunit of a *stride* including four footprints (two fronts and two hinds, and two lefts and two rights). The measure of the group plus the intergroup equals the measure of the stride.

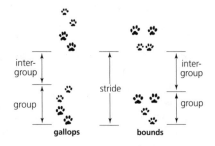

half bound:
See *bound*.

heel: portion of foot or track to the rear of digital and interdigital pads. In mammals, may be covered with hair, naked (without hair), or have one or more proximal pads. In reptiles and amphibians, may be textured with *tubercles*.

hop: synonymous with bound, often used in reference to gaits of rodents and rabbits.

indented lobe: See *fringe*.

interdigital pad: See *pad*.

length: of a track, the distance from front of toe *pads* to back of the interdigital pads, measured parallel to the *foot axis*. In mammal tracks, does not include claws. In bird tracks, does not include toe 1, but includes claws if they are attached and indistinguishable from toe pad.

line of travel: imaginary line on the ground over which the center of gravity of an animal passes.

lobe: See *fringe*.

lope: a slow *gallop*, in which at least one hind foot registers behind a front foot in a group of four footprints. See illustration on page xxv.

mesial webbing: See *webbing*.

minimum outline: See pages xix–xx for extended discussion.

nipple-dimple: See *scat shape*.

outer toe angle: in birds, the angle between toes 2 and 4. In perching birds less than 90° and in shorebirds greater than 120°.

oval: See *scat shape*.

pad: hard, calluslike structure on the side of the sole of an animal's foot. Each toe may have a digital pad. One or more interdigital pads are located directly to the rear of the toes, and one or more proximal pads may be located directly to the rear of the interdigital pads. In deer and their relatives, there is a single pad separated from the *wall* by the *sub-unguinis*. In birds, a metatarsal pad may occur directly under the leg bone.

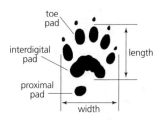

plantigrade: walking on the soles of the foot. Raccoons, bears, and humans, for example, are plantigrade. The sole of the foot usually shows in the footprint. Compare to *digitigrade*.

pronk: a *gait* in which all four feet strike the ground simultaneously and directly below the body. The *group* pattern shows two front footprints ahead of the two hind prints. Also called a *stot*. See illustration on page xxiii.

proximal pad: See *pad*.

proximal webbing: See *webbing*.

rotatory gallop: a type of *gallop* that tends to form a C-shaped *group* pattern. See illustration on page xxii.

run: a *gait* used when moving only on two legs. It differs from a *walk* in having a longer *stride*.

scat shape: *Cords* are long pieces of scat, typically four to ten times longer than the width. Ends may be blunt or tapered. *Ovals* are pieces of scat typically two to four times longer than wide and tapered at both ends. A *nipple-dimple* shaped scat pellet has a point on one end and a depression at the other. See chart on page xviii.

simple fringe, simple lobe: See *fringe*.

sole: bottom of an animal's foot. It may be covered with hair or naked, and may have one or more *pads* on it.

stot

stot: See *pronk*.

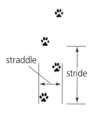

straddle: the distance from the right edge of the rightmost pad to the leftmost edge of the leftmost pad in a *trail*. Measure at right angles to the *line of travel*.

stride: The distance from the point where a foot touches the ground to the point where the same foot touches the ground again. Measured parallel to the *line of travel*. One stride is equal to a *group* plus and intergroup measurement.

subunguinis: the soft material under the nails of humans. In deer and their relatives, refers specifically to the soft material between the *pad* and *wall*.

symmetrical: having two sides, one the mirror image of the other side.

toe pad: See *pad*.

track: refers to an individual footprint. Some measurable characteristics include *length* and *width*.

track pattern: the gross visual image of the pattern of footprints on the ground. A repeating pattern of two prints separated from the next two is called two-by and written 2 x 2. Prints may also show patterns of 3 x 3, 4 x 4, and 1 x 2 x 1. These patterns are made during a *gallop* or a *bound*. A few of these patterns are illustrated on page xxii–xxiii.

trail: a series of footprints and associated sign that marks the passage of an animal. Some measurable characteristics include *stride* and *straddle*.

traverse gallop: a type of *gallop* that tends to form a Z-shaped group pattern. See illustration on page xxii.

trot: a *gait* in which evenly spaced footprints alternate on right and left sides of the *line of travel*. Hind footprint registers on top of front. As speed increases, hind moves forward of front. Same patterns as a *walk*, but longer *stride*. May be done with body turned to side. See illustration on page xxii.

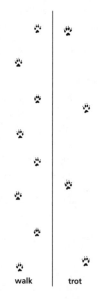

walk | trot

tubercle: rough pinhead-sized protuberance on the sole of the foot of a reptile or amphibian.

unguinis: hard material forming nails in humans, hoof walls in deer and their relatives, and claws in other mammals. Composed of hair pasted together by body glues.

walk: a *gait* where evenly spaced footprints alternate on right and left sides of the *line of travel*. Hind footprint registers on top of front. As speed increases, hind moves forward of front. See illustrations on pages xxii and xxv.

wall: hard material around the edge of each clout of a hoof. Technically the *unguinis*, which also forms human nails and animal claws.

webbing: thin membrane stretched between toes of animals. The webbing may be near the tips of the toes (*distal*), and midway to the toe tips (*mesial*), or attached at the base (*proximal*). A membrane attached to only one toe is called a *fringe*.

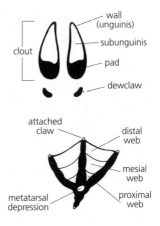

width: of a track, the greatest distance from the right side of the pads of a foot to the left side, whether the greatest distance is across the toes or palm pads. Measured perpendicular to the *foot axis*. In bird tracks, includes claws if they are attached and indistinguishable from toe pad.

How to use *Scats and Tracks*

Scats and Tracks of the Southeast is designed for easy use in the field. The gray bars found on the edges of the pages of the track accounts will help you measure scat diameter and footprint size; each of these bars is keyed to the average size of the sign in question. A ruler is provided on the back cover. Below, we provide the background knowledge that every tracker should be familiar with before going to the field or using this book. Please take some time to study this material.

Illustrations

Illustrator Todd Telander applied his great ability to our collections of plaster casts, photographs, and slides, drawing on our experience to produce the most up-to-date and accurate illustrations possible. These drawings—made from the best specimens in a collection of thousands—represent the culmination of decades of tracking experience and are far more accurate than the tracker usually finds in tracking books. The tracks you find on the ground may not have as much detail or be as clear, but it is better to have an excellent drawing to compare to an imperfect track than to have to compare a track to a drawing lacking critical details.

How to use the track accounts

The track accounts in this guide have been grouped by similar footprint characteristics. Each track account represents a single species or a group of species with similar track characteristics. Each account is presented across a two-page spread and is conveniently divided into sections as discussed below. A brief listing of visual characteristics used to identify an animal begins each track account, appearing beneath the common and scientific names of the species. These descriptions are general, and great variability of pattern can exist among animals in the field. We recommend consulting appropriate field identification guides.

Track: A concise description of key points of footprints, to be used for identification. The accompanying track illustrations are not at actual size; unless otherwise noted, actual (average) length of the footprint is shown as a bar on the right side of the right-hand page. Average width is shown as a bar on the bottom of the right-hand page. In the field, place the appropriate measurement bar next to the track to compare size. To take a numerical measurement, use the ruler printed on the back cover of the book.

The tracks illustrated are all from right feet, except in the entries for birds, where both feet are pictured. Numerical measurements are given in the form *length x width*. Notes that measurements of mammal tracks do not include claws, that measurements of bird tracks include claws but do not include toe 1, and that measurements generally do not include parts of the foot that often do not register in a given specie's track (e.g., heels in the hind feet of some rodent species).

Trail: The average size of the stride of the most commonly used gait or gaits is given. Other common or characteristic gaits, if any, are discussed. See *track patterns* in the Glossary of Terms on page xxx. For more information on gaits in tracking, see *A Field Guide to Mammal Tracking in North America* by Jim Halfpenny (1986). Gaits are displayed up the right side of the right-hand page. If the common gait is a walk or trot, however, it may not be illustrated, since all walking and trotting patterns consist of right-left alternating patterns.

Scat: A description of scat supplements the drawing. Average scat width is shown as a bar up the side of the left-hand page. In the field, place the appropriate meas-urement bar next to the scat to compare sizes. To take a numerical measurement, use the ruler printed on the back cover of the book. Numerical measurements of scat are given under the illustrations in the form *length x width*. In cases of small scat, only width is given; thus, a single measurement always indicates diameter.

Habitat: To aid in locating and differentiating tracks, the animal's habitat preferences are listed. Some animals with large ranges, such as the beaver, are found only in specific habitats.

Similar species: Clues are provided to help differenti-ate an animal's tracks from similar tracks of other species. With these clues, identification should be possible.

Other sign: Other sign of animals, beside tracks and scat, are listed or illustrated to help with identification, and simply to provide more information on animal lives.

In addition, a distribution map is provided with each account. This gives a generalized picture of where in the Southeast region an animal may be found. Animals that require specific habitats will of course not be evenly dis-tributed through the shown range.

To make the best use of this guide, carry it with you into the field. When you come across an unfamiliar track or trail, open the book to the appropriate track account and place the page alongside the track for immediate on-site comparison.

Visual key to tracks

This simple key includes birds, reptiles, amphibians, and mammals. It is arranged by the number of toes that show in a good footprint, ranging from no toes to two toes to five toes. Those animals that show four toes in the front print and five toes in the hind are listed between four- and five-toed animals.

Fiddler and Horseshoe Crabs (pp. 2–5)

Two to several parallel series of holes in the ground. Trail may be 1 to 12 inches (2.5 to 30 cm) wide and include shell drag marks.

Snakes (pp. 30–31)

Series of side-to-side trail undulations.

Deer and Relatives (pp. 138–41)

Two toes form hard, cloven hoof. Dewclaws may show in deep print.

Birds with Webbed Feet (pp. 32–47)

Three toes facing forward, often a fourth toe facing backward. Claws may be detached from toes. Webbing between two or more toes.

Birds without Webbed Feet (pp. 48–71)

Three toes facing forward, often a fourth toe facing backward. Claws may be detached from toes.

Wolves, Dogs, and Relatives (pp. 78–83)

Four toes in front and hind prints. Claws usually present and detached. Single anterior lobe on interdigital pad.

Cats and Relatives (pp. 84–89)

Four toes in front and hind prints. Claws usually absent. Double anterior lobe on interdigital pad.

Rabbits and Relatives (pp. 108–11)

Four toes in front and hind footprint. An exceptionally clear print may show a fifth inner toe in the front footprint. Pads lacking, bottom of foot covered with hair. Long hopping heel in hind print.

Armadillo (pp. 74–75)

Four toes in front print and five toes in hind. Often only the prominent inner toes—two on front, three on hind—register.

Salamanders (pp. 6–9)

Four toes in front print, five toes in hind. Trail wide, often with a tail drag.

Frogs (pp. 12–17)

Four toes in front print, five toes in hind. Long, slender toes. Front print faces center of trail. Distal webbing in hind print.

Toads (pp. 10–11)

Four toes in front print, five toes in hind. Front print faces center of trail. Mesial webbing in hind print. Tubercles may show on front and hind prints.

Rodents (pp. 112–37)

Most have four toes in front prints and five in hind. Beaver has five toes in front print. Front toes show a 1-2-1 grouping; hind show a 1-3-1 grouping. Long hopping heel in hind print.

Lizards (pp. 26–29)

Five toes in front and hind prints. Toes long and slender. Claws may be detached. Tail drag often present in trail.

Turtles (pp. 20–25)

Five toes show in front and hind tracks. Front prints toe-in and hind prints may toe-out. Feet are relatively broad. Claws robust and often visible. Sometimes the claws are the only visible signs on hard ground.

Opossum (pp. 72–73)

Five toes. Distinct hind print with an opposable (like human thumb) inside toe protruding sideways from other toes. Outside toe is slightly separated from middle three toes.

Shrews (pp. 76–77)

Five slender toes present on front and hind feet. In clear prints, four interdigital and two proximal pads may be seen.

Raccoons and Relatives (pp. 92–95)

Five toes in front and hind prints. Toes often round or bulbous at ends. May have long, slender toes.

Weasels and Relatives (pp. 96–107)

Five toes in front and hind prints, though the little toe (on inside of foot) may not show. Toes in a 1-3-1 grouping. Interdigital pad is chevron-shaped. Plantigrade hind foot.

Black Bear (pp. 90–92)

Five toes in front and hind prints, though the little toe (on inside of foot) may not show. Toes evenly spaced. Plantigrade hind foot.

Scats
and
Tracks
of the

Southeast

Fiddler Crab
Uca pugilator

Small crab with squarish shell that tapers at back and lacks notch on edge. Eye stalk longer than space between eyes. Males have one large claw, females two small claws.

Track: Each foot creates a simple small hole, which in very wet sand may be slightly elongated.

Trail: Series of roundish holes in roughly parallel lines. Stride varies from 0.1 to 0.3 inch (0.3 to 0.8 cm). Straddle varies from 0.75 to 1.0 inch (1.8 to 2.5 cm). Because the crab moves sideways, its eight feet create four lines of holes, but as the crab turns, the number of lines increases to eight lines.

Scat: Not known.

hole in sand with tracks

Habitat: Sand beaches to muddy beaches for similar species. Burrows in area between tide marks.

Similar species: Footprint holes of ghost crabs usually elongate and they leave wider trails, about 4 inches (10 cm). Parallel rows of dot-like tracks separate fiddler trails from all other species.

Other sign: Domed entrances to burrows and balls of sand excavated from the burrow.

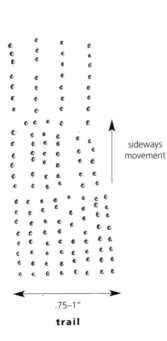

sideways
movement

.75–1"

trail

Horseshoe Crab
Limulus polyphemus

Unmistakable hard horseshoe-shaped shell with tail spike. May reach 24 inches (61 cm) in length. Not a crab but a relative of spiders.

Track: Walking feet consist of two elongate holes about 0.75 inch (1.9 cm) wide form an inverted "V." Rarely small hind feet register and look like ski pole baskets.

Trail: A wide, 10 to 12 inch (25 to 30 cm), drag mark through the sand consisting of two parallel rows of foot holes inside the shell drag mark. Distance between holes is about 2 inches (5 cm). Tail drags down the middle of the trail.

egg mass on sandy beach

Scat: Not known.

Habitat: Intertidal to subtidal zones.

Similar species: Broad trail with footprint and trail drag is distinctive from other species.

Other sign: Series of round nest mounds where round, green eggs are deposited. Eggs occasionally exposed by water.

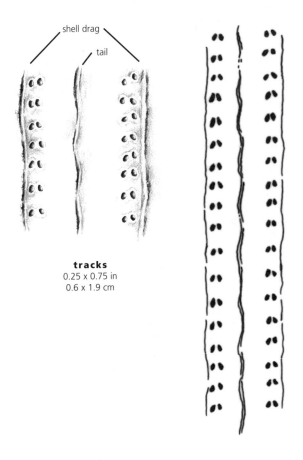

tracks
0.25 x 0.75 in
0.6 x 1.9 cm

Eastern Newt—Red Eft phase
Notophthalmus viridescens

Vienna sausage-sized
salamander, up to 4
inches (10 cm) long.
Moist, smooth skin.
Terrestrial form, called
red eft, is bright orange-red with red spots outlined in black.
Tubercles on underside of foot.

Track: Four toes on front foot (often only three show) and five toes on hind foot. The outline of the foot may not show, just toe prints. Even in a clear print, tubercles rarely show.

Trail: Walking stride is about 1 inch (2.5 cm). Trail has a wide straddle 0.67 inch (1.6 cm) relative to stride and may show oscillating belly and tail drag marks.

Scat: Brown to black with slightly tapered ends.

scat
0.23 x 0.09 in
0.6 x 0.3 cm

SCAT WIDTH

Habitat: Quiet waters around lakes, ponds, and streams in grassland meadow areas and forests.

Similar species: Differs from lizards by wider, oscillating tail drag (if present) and by having only four toes on front foot. Considerably smaller tracks and trail than most salamanders.

Other sign: Eggs mass found in water along shore.

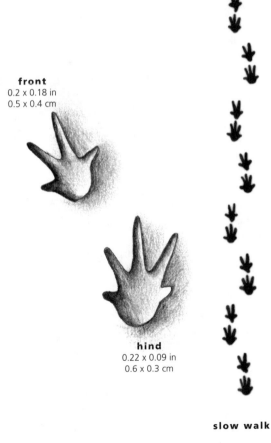

front
0.2 x 0.18 in
0.5 x 0.4 cm

hind
0.22 x 0.09 in
0.6 x 0.3 cm

slow walk

FRONT TRACK LENGTH

FRONT TRACK WIDTH

Tiger Salamander
Ambystoma tigrinum

Hot dog–sized salamander, up to 9 inches (23 cm) long. Moist, smooth skin. Body brown to black to dark green, with yellow spots or streaks. Tubercles on underside of foot.

Track: Four toes on front foot (often only three show) and five toes on hind foot. The outline of the foot may not show, just toe prints. Even in a clear print, tubercles rarely show.

Trail: Walking stride is about 3 inches (7.5 cm). Trail has a wide straddle relative to stride and may show oscillating belly and tail drag marks.

Scat: Soft, pea-sized black masses with some hint of oval shape.

Habitat: Quiet waters around lakes, ponds, and streams in grassland meadow areas and forests.

scat
0.3 x 0.2 in
0.7 x 0.6 cm

egg mass

SCAT WIDTH

Similar species: Differs from lizards by wider, oscillating tail drag and by having only four toes on front foot. Larger tracks and trail than newts.

Other sign: Eggs in egg masses are attached individually to underwater plant stems.

front
0.6 x 0.3 in
1.5 x 0.8 cm

hind
0.8 x 0.6 in
2 x 1.5 cm

slow walk

FRONT TRACK LENGTH

FRONT TRACK WIDTH

American Toad
Bufo americanus

Baseball-sized toad, up
to 3.5 inches (9 cm)
long. Body is plain
brown to gray to reddish,
with warts from yellow to
red in dark brown or black
spots. A white line runs down
the back. Only one or two large
warts in each dark spot. Female larger than male.

Track: Four toes on
front foot and five
on hind. Front
feet face in.
Two tubercles
on heel of front
foot. Three hind toes
face in, one forward, and
one out. Two tubercles may

show on the heel of the hind foot and can be confused with
toes. Webbing, found only on hind
feet, extends at most halfway out
to toe tips.

scat
0.9 x 0.2 in
2.3 x 0.5 cm

egg mass

**toad imprint
in mud**

SCAT WIDTH

Trail: Hopping or full bound stride generally 5 to 7 inches (13 to 18 cm). Walking stride is about 2.5 inches (7.5 cm).

Scat: Dark brown to black. Long cord, up to five times longer than wide. Sometimes contains insect parts.

Habitat: Lakes, ponds, beaver ponds, and wet mixed coniferous forest.

Similar species: Differs from frogs by presence of tubercles on front heels. Hind foot is narrower than frog. Walks and uses short hops more than the usually long-hopping frog.

Other sign: Long strings of egg masses on bottom of water source and floating among vegetation.

walk

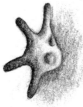

front
0.8 x 0.5 in
2 x 1.3 cm

mesial web

hind
1 x 0.9 in
2.5 x 2.3 cm

hop

FRONT TRACK LENGTH

FRONT TRACK WIDTH

Chorus Frog
Pseudacris triseriata

Silver dollar–sized frog less than 1.5 inches (3.8 cm). Highly variable frog with body color from brown to green. Darker stripe pattern varies with subspecies.

Track: Four toes on front foot and five on hind. Front feet face in. Four hind toes face in, with one facing out. Proximal webbing on hind feet extending at most one-quarter of way out to toe tips.

Trail: Hopping stride about 10 inches (25 cm). Frogs may easily hop 3 feet (1 m) when in a hurry.

Scat: Black, firm cord with slightly tapering ends.

scat
0.5 x 0.1 in
1.3 x 0.3 cm

egg mass and tadpole

SCAT WIDTH

Habitat: Shallow water with emergent vegetation, including pond and lake shores, marshes, and beaver ponds.

Similar species: Lacks the palm tubercles of the front feet of toad. Less webbing between toes. Hops more and longer distances. Smaller than leopard frog.

Other sign: Inconspicuous egg masses consisting of a few eggs in a packet attached to vegetation below waterline.

front
0.6 x 0.4 in
1.5 x 1 cm

walk

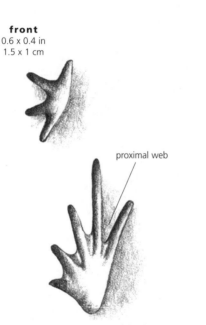

proximal web

hind
0.8 x 0.6 in
2 x 1.5 cm

hop

FRONT TRACK LENGTH

FRONT TRACK WIDTH

Leopard Frog
Rana utricularia

Baseball-sized frog, up to
inches (9 cm) long. Body
light to dark brown or
green, with dark spots.
Spots have light borders.
Head relatively long and
pointed. White stripe on
jaw. Often a light spot on
eardrum.

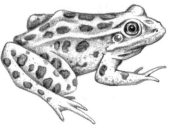

Track: Four toes on
front foot and five
on hind. Front
feet face in.
Four hind toes
face in, with one
facing out. Web-
bing, found only on hind
feet, is distal, extending
most of the way out to toe tips. Toe 1 is thick on male
because it serves as the nuptial pad for grasping female during
mating.

scat
1.5 x 0.4 in
3.8 x 1 cm

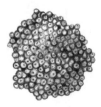

egg mass

SCAT WIDTH

Trail: Full bound or hopping stride is about 20 inches (50 cm). May easily hop 3 feet (1 m) when in a hurry. Occasionally walk.

Scat: Brown to black, with slightly tapered ends.

Habitat: Cold, nonseasonal ponds, streams, and other water sources. May be found in meadows well away from water.

Similar species: Nuptial pad (enlarged pad for holding female during mating) separates male from other hopping amphibians. Differs from toads by more webbing between toes, lack of palm tubercles on front feet, and by hopping more and at longer distances. Larger than chorus frogs.

Other sign: Softball-sized egg masses floating just below water surface.

walk

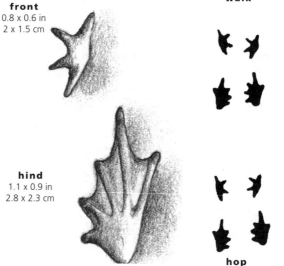

front
0.8 x 0.6 in
2 x 1.5 cm

hind
1.1 x 0.9 in
2.8 x 2.3 cm

hop

FRONT TRACK LENGTH

FRONT TRACK WIDTH

Bullfrog
Rana catesbeiana

Softball-sized frog, 4 to 8 inches (10 to 20 cm) long. Brownish green to green, becoming light green on head. Legs banded with dark brown to green; small spots on back. Fold of skin around eye and large expose eardrum.

Track: Four toes on front foot and five on hind. Front feet face in. Three hind toes face in, remaining two face forward or out. Webbing, found only on hind feet, is distal, extending most of the way out to the toe tips. In a clear track, a male's toe 2 (thumb) on front foot appears thicker at base.

Trail: Hopping stride is 24 inches (60 cm). May easily hop 72 inches (180 cm).

scat
1.5 x 0.4 in
3.8 x 1 cm

SCAT WIDTH

Scat: Brown to black, with slightly tapered ends.

Habitat: Permanent and (usually) quiet water with dense growth of aquatic plants, especially cattails, in plains, woodlands, and forest.

Similar species: Differs from toads by more webbing between toes, lack of palm tubercles on front feet, and by hopping more and at longer distances. Differs from leopard frog and chorus frogs by larger feet.

Other sign: Deposits a globular egg mass.

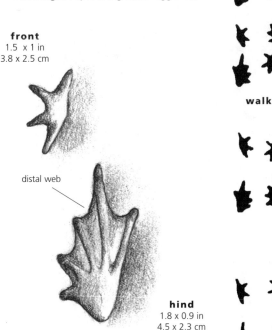

front
1.5 x 1 in
3.8 x 2.5 cm

distal web

hind
1.8 x 0.9 in
4.5 x 2.3 cm

walk

hop

FRONT TRACK LENGTH

FRONT TRACK WIDTH

Alligator
Alligator mississippiensis

Roughly the size
of a short tele-
phone pole, body
varying from 5 to 15 feet
or more (1.5 to 4.5 m), with
dry skin and ridged scales. Black to dark gray body. Broad
rounded snout distinguishes it from a crocodile.

Track: Five toes on
front foot. Inside
and outside
toes are oppo-
site and form a
straight line.
Four toes on hind
foot with a well-devel-
oped heel. Claws
detached. Skin tubercles may show in the bottom of
the tracks. Tracks size varies considerably because alligators continue to grow their entire life.

Trail: Walking stride is about 40 inches (100 cm), but this varies
with alligator size.

Scat: We have not observed their scat.

Habitat: Prefers river swamps, marshes, and bayous.

Similar species: No similar tracks for adults. Young might be confused with turtles, but have four toes on hind feet.

Other sign: Nest composed of vegetation and may be up to 7 feet (2.1 m) in diameter and 3 feet (90 cm) high.

front
about 6.75 x 8 in
about 17 x 20 cm

hind
about 11 x 9 in
about 28 x 23 cm

FRONT TRACK LENGTH (50%)

FRONT TRACK WIDTH (50%)

Painted Turtle
Chrysemys picta

A small turtle with
smooth, unkeeled
shells and patterns of
red, yellow, and black.
Length to 8 inches (20 cm).
Females larger than males.

Track: Five toes with
claws show in front
and back
prints. Claws
longer on front
feet and those of
the male's front feet
are two to three times
longer than the female's.

Outer toe on hind foot lacks claw. Distal webbing on front and
hind prints.

Trail: Walking stride averages 4.5 inches (11.5 cm) with a straddle of 4 inches (10 cm). Front feet toe in and hind feet toe out.
Hind footprint registers slightly behind. Tail drag often visible.

Scat: Usually black semiliquid, slightly elongated clumps.

scat
0.9 x 0.2 in
1.3 x 0.5 cm

SCAT WIDTH

Habitat: Ponds, lakes, marshes, swamps, streams, and ditches with abundant vegetation.

Similar species: Differs from snapping turtles by its narrow straight trail.

Other sign: Nests are usually dug in sand in open areas where sun warms eggs.

front
0.8 x 0.7 in without claws
2 x 1.8 cm

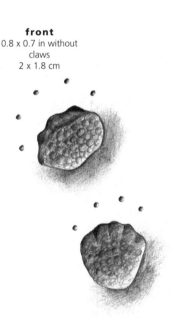

hind
1.1 x 1.0 in without claws
2.8 x 2.5 cm

walk

FRONT TRACK LENGTH

FRONT TRACK WIDTH

Snapping Turtle
Chelydra serpentina

A large to very large turtle,
average weight 10
to 30 pounds
(4.5 to 16 kg).
The robust shell
is lined by three toothed
ridges. Large head with
robust, hooked jaw. Tail longer than half the shell and
toothed on top.

Track: Five toes show
in front and
hind tracks.
Front prints toe
in and hind prints
may toe out. Feet
are relatively broad.
Claws robust and often
visible. Sometimes the claws are the only visible sign on
hard ground.

Trail: Walking stride ranges from 5 to 12 inches (12.5 to 30 cm).
Straddle is wide compared to stride. Tail drag often present.

Scat: Lacks well-defined shape. Color is algae green to dark black.
Often soft.

scat
1.5 in
3.8 cm

SCAT WIDTH

Habitat: Always near water, including swamps, marshes, lakes, streams, and rivers.

Similar species: Broad trail of five-toed, clawed track with a tail drag separates the snapping turtle tracks and trail.

Other sign: Nest in open area where sun warms sand and eggs. Nest may be several inches deep.

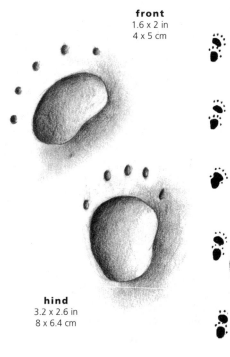

front
1.6 x 2 in
4 x 5 cm

hind
3.2 x 2.6 in
8 x 6.4 cm

slow walk

FRONT TRACK LENGTH

FRONT TRACK WIDTH

Atlantic Loggerhead Turtle
Caretta caretta

A very large sea
turtle, weighing
170 to 350 pounds
(80 to 160 kg). Reddish-
brown color with five or
more coastal (side) plates.

Track: Flipper-shaped limbs with
two claws leave two
holes in the sand. In
hard sand,
only the front
end of the
flipper may
show. Prints may
be obliterated by the
dragging motion of
front legs scraping the sand.
Hind feet often only a drag mark.

Trail: Walking stride about 12 inches (30 cm). Straddle is wide
compared to stride, 28 to 36 inches (70 to 90 cm). Front feet,
which sweep backward and in, register well outside the shell drag
mark, which is 8 to 12 inches (20 to 30 cm) wide. Front feet may
push up mounds of sand. Hind feet often show only as drag
marks.

sand mound with flipper kick marks

Scat: Not known; turtle defecates in water.

Habitat: Ocean beaches.

Similar species: Broad dragging trail of shell with parallel rows of two holes on each side of shell drag mark separates sea turtles from other turtles.

Other sign: Nests 12 inches (30 cm) deep are dug in beach sand.

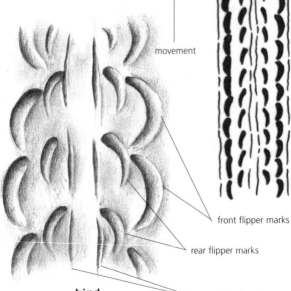

front
6 to 10 x 3 to 6 in
15 to 25 x 7.5 to 15 cm

movement

front flipper marks

rear flipper marks

hind
6 to 8 x 5 to 7 in
15 to 20 x 12.5 to 18 cm

bottom of shell marks

FRONT TRACK LENGTH

FRONT TRACK WIDTH

Texas Horned Lizard
Phrynosoma cornutum

Roughly the size of a call
ing card; body and tail le
than 4 inches (10 cm)
long. Body relatively
broad, with horns pro-
jecting from back of head
Central two head spines
longer than others. Body
brown to tan, closely matching local terrain
colors. Two rows of fringe scales along edge of body.

Track: Five relatively long, thin toes on front and hind feet. Hind heel is relatively long. Claws may show.

Trail: Trotting stride is 3 inches (7.5 cm). Hind feet mostly register on top of front feet. Relatively wide straddle. Relatively straight tail drag and often a wider body drag.

Scat: Brown pellets three to six times longer than wide; may be tapered. White nitrogenous material may be found on one end.

scat
1.5 x 0.25 in
3.8 x 0.6 cm

SCAT WIDTH

Habitat: Determined by presence of fine, loose soil interspersed with firm, sandy or rocky terrain. Found in prairies and open woodlands, from plains high into mountains.

Similar species: Differs from salamanders by having five narrow toes on front feet and relatively straight tail drag. Differs from fence lizard by wider footprint.

Other sign: Scuff marks in loose sand where the lizard buries itself for camouflage.

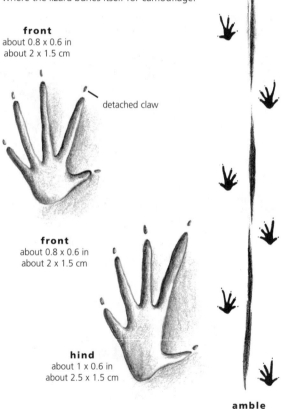

front
about 0.8 x 0.6 in
about 2 x 1.5 cm

detached claw

front
about 0.8 x 0.6 in
about 2 x 1.5 cm

hind
about 1 x 0.6 in
about 2.5 x 1.5 cm

amble

FRONT TRACK LENGTH

FRONT TRACK WIDTH

Northern Fence Lizard
Sceloporus undulatus

Roughly the size of a roll of Life Savers; body about 3 inches (7.5 cm), with dry skin and ridged scales. Gray to dark brown above, with black crossbars or longitudinal stripes. Blue patches surrounded by black on side of throat. Considerable subspecies variation.

Track: Five relatively long, thin toes on front and hind feet. Hind heel is relatively long. Claws may show.

Trail: Trotting stride is about 3 inches (7.5). Hind feet mostly register on top of front feet. Relatively wide straddle. Straight tail drag.

Scat: Brown cord, up to six to eight times longer than wide. White nitrogenous material usually found on one end.

Habitat: Wide variety of habitats, including forests, woodland, and rock outcrops. Shelters in bushes, trees, or logs or under rocks.

scat
1.5 x 0.25 in
3.8 x 0.6 cm

SCAT WIDTH

Similar species: Differs from salamanders by having five narrow toes on front feet and straighter tail drag. Differs from horned lizard by narrower footprint.

Other sign: Scuff marks in dust may indicate a dust bath.

detached claw

front
0.8 x 0.25 in
2 x 0.6 cm

hind
1 x 0.3 in
2.5 x 0.8 cm

slow walk

FRONT TRACK LENGTH

FRONT TRACK WIDTH

Snakes
various species

A variety of snakes,
from garter snakes
(*Thamnophis sirtalis*) to milk snakes
(*Lampropeltis triangulum*) to
rattlesnakes (*Crotalus horridus*).

Rattlesnake
Crotalus horridus

Track: No footprint to describe.

Trail: Varies from 1 to 4 inches (2.5 to 10 cm) wide. Characterized by side-to-side undulations of the trail. The period, the distance from one curve to the next, varies by species, age, and speed of the snake. Surface material is usually pushed up at the outside of each curve. Gait is either a side-to-side undulation or sidewinding.

Scat: Black or brown cord, with constrictions and undulations. White nitrogenous material often attached.

scat
4 x 0.4 in
20 x 1 cm

shed skin

Habitat: Varies widely—from water's edge to rock outcrops to dry sand dunes.

Similar species: Resembles no other track.

Other sign: Shed skin.

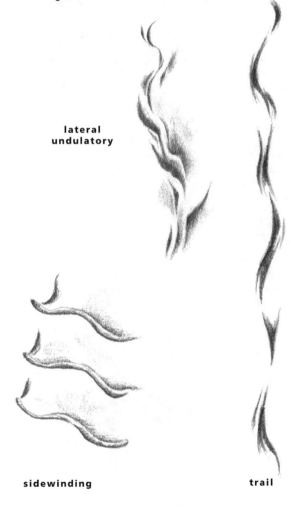

lateral undulatory

sidewinding

trail

Common Loon
Gavia immer

Large-sized, long-bodied aquatic bird, average length 24 inches (60 cm). Dark-colored bird with black and white checkered back and neck band. Dark greenish head.

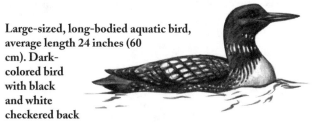

Track: Three toes showing, toes 2 to 4 pointing forward. Toe 1 does not register. Toes 2, 3, and 4 have claws and distal webbing.

Trail: Walking stride is 10 inches (25 cm) with a 7-inch (18-cm) straddle. Toes turn inward. Foot drag marks usually evident because the loon's legs are placed far back on its body, making walking difficult and causing the loon to drag its feet.

Scat: Not known.

nest

SCAT WIDTH

Habitat: Freshwater lakes and rivers; near shore on ocean.

Similar species: Differs from all other aquatic birds by heavy drag marks in trail and relatively long, narrow feet.

Other sign: Large nest on reeds and brush at edge of water. Eggs appear large in small nest.

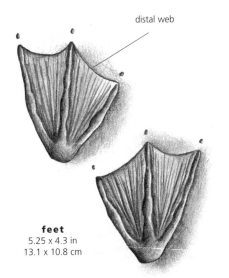

distal web

feet
5.25 x 4.3 in
13.1 x 10.8 cm

walk

FRONT TRACK LENGTH (50%)

FRONT TRACK WIDTH (50%)

White Pelican
Pelecanus erythrorhynchos

Large aquatic bird, average length more than 60 inches (150 cm), with a wingspan of more than 8 feet (2.4 m). White with black primary wing feathers. Large bill is yellow to orange.

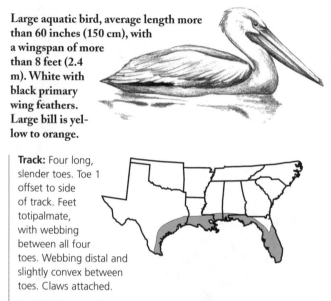

Track: Four long, slender toes. Toe 1 offset to side of track. Feet totipalmate, with webbing between all four toes. Webbing distal and slightly convex between toes. Claws attached.

Trail: Walking stride averages 16 inches (40 cm). Toes turn inward.

ground nest

SCAT WIDTH

Scat: Shapeless, brownish-white mass.

Habitat: Lakes, marshes, and bays. During summer, found in freshwater lakes; in winter, found in salt water.

Similar species: Differs from all other web-footed birds except cormorant by being totipalmate. Differs from cormorant by having attached claws.

Other sign: Nests on ground in large island colonies.

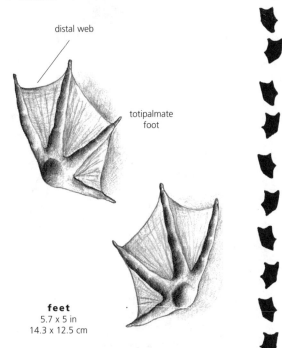

distal web

totipalmate foot

feet
5.7 x 5 in
14.3 x 12.5 cm

walk

Double-crested Cormorant
Phalacrocorax auritus

Large aquatic bird, average length more than 32 inches (80 cm), with a wingspan of more than 4.3 feet (132 cm). Dark-colored body with orange throat patch. Crest of two white feathers behind eye, which may be difficult to see.

Track: Four long, slender toes. Toe 1 offset to side of track. Toe 4 is longest. Feet *totipalmate*, i.e.,with webbing between all four toes. Webbing distal and slightly convex between toes. Claws detached.

Trail: Walking stride is about 10 inches (25 cm). Walks awkwardly on land, with a short stride for its size. Toes turn inward.

nest

Scat: Shapeless, nearly liquid white mass.

Habitat: Saltwater islands, bays, and cliffs. Freshwater lakes, ponds, and swamps.

Similar species: Differs from all other web-footed birds except pelican by being totipalmate. Differs from pelican by having detached claws.

Other sign: Nests in colonies on ground or in trees. Acidic scat kills trees and ground vegetation.

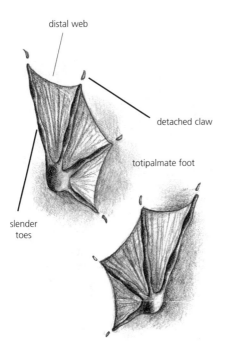

distal web

detached claw

totipalmate foot

slender toes

feet
up to 5.2 x 4.8 in
up to 13 x 12 cm

walk

FRONT TRACK LENGTH (50%)

FRONT TRACK WIDTH (50%)

Green-backed Heron
Butorides striatus

Medium-sized wading bird, average length 14 inches (36 cm). Male and female similar in overall appearance: blue to greenish body, with reddish-brown neck and yellowish legs.

Track: Four toes, toes 2 to 4 pointing forward. Small proximal web between toes 3 and 4. Footprint is asymmetrical, with toe 1 set to inside of foot axis (drawn through toe 3). On hard ground, metatarsal pad may not show (that is, toes may appear unconnected).

cough pellet

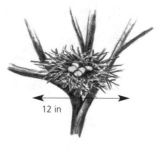

12 in

nest
4–5 eggs common

Trail: Walking stride about 10 inches (25 cm). Trail is fairly straight and feet point forward.

Scat: Semiliquid, predominantly white. Solid cords of scat vary from 1 to 3 inches (2.5 to 5 cm) and may contain fish, insects, frogs, and salamanders.

Habitat: Freshwater and saltwater areas along ponds, streams, lakes, swamps, and beaches where heavily wooded.

Similar species: Smaller version of great blue heron track (6.5 in/ 16.5 cm). Differs from other shore-edge tracks by asymmetrical placement of toes.

Other sign: Undigested material may be coughed up as pellets.

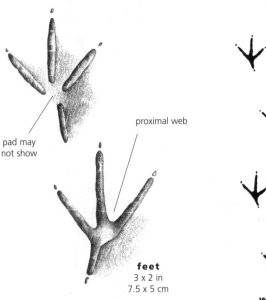

pad may not show

proximal web

feet
3 x 2 in
7.5 x 5 cm

walk

Great Blue Heron
Ardea herodias

Large wading bird, average length 45 inches (113 cm). Male and female similar in overall appearance: gray-blue body, with white neck and yellow beak. Black crown extends on feathers off rear of head.

Track: Four toes, toes 2 to 4 pointing forward. Small proximal web between toes 3 and 4. Footprint is asymmetrical, with toe 1 set to inside of foot axis (drawn through toe 3). Toe 1 is about 1.5 inches (3.8 cm); toe 2 is longer than 1, though shorter than 3 and 4. On hard ground, metatarsal pad may not show (that is, toes may appear unconnected).

cough pellet

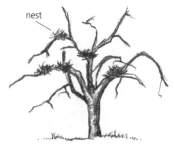

nest

rookery

Trail: Walking stride about 20 inches (50 cm). Trail is fairly straight and feet point forward.

Scat: Semiliquid, predominantly white. Solid cords of scat vary from 2 to 3 inches (5 to 7.5 cm) in length, and may contain fish, frogs, salamanders, and even small rodents. Ground beneath nests becomes coated with droppings.

Habitat: Frequents backwater eddies along riverbanks, shallow edges of lakes, and tide-flats.

Similar species: Differs from other shore-edge tracks by large size and asymmetrical placement of toes.

Other sign: Large colonies of nests high in trees. Undigested material may be coughed up as pellets.

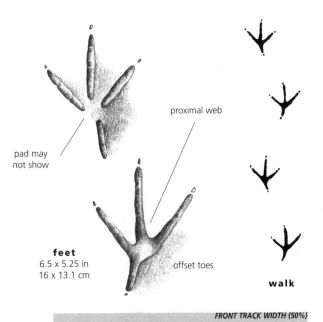

proximal web

pad may not show

feet
6.5 x 5.25 in
16 x 13.1 cm

offset toes

walk

FRONT TRACK LENGTH (50%)

FRONT TRACK WIDTH (50%)

Sandhill Crane
Grus canadensis

Large bird, average length 39 inches
(98 cm). Appearance of males and
females similar: grayish, with red
crown on head, and white cheeks and
chin.

Track: Four toes, toes 2 to 4 showing. Outside
toes opposed by nearly 180 degrees. Toe 3 is
longer than 2 and 4. Small proximal web
between toes 2 and 3 rarely shows. Claws
usually attached to toes, though claw of
toe 1 rarely shows. Feet point forward.

Trail: Walking stride
about 24 inches
(60 cm). Often
runs, extending
its stride. Tracks
have a narrow
straddle, being
nearly in line with each
other.

Scat: Similar to, but smaller than, Canada goose. Brown in color,
with some vegetation. Can contain bones of small mammals, reptiles, and amphibians.

scat
2.5 x 0.3 in
6.3 x 8 cm

SCAT WIDTH

Habitat: Meadows, marshes, grasslands, and fields.

Similar species: Differs from ducks, geese, swans, and herons by having only small proximal web. Differs from large raptors by lacking toe 1.

Other sign: Listen for its rattling call, which suggests to some what dinosaurs may have sounded like.

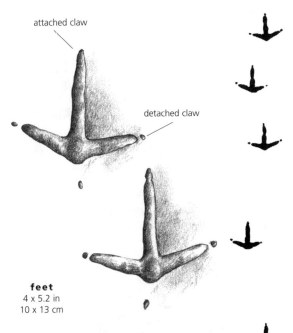

attached claw

detached claw

feet
4 x 5.2 in
10 x 13 cm

walk

FRONT TRACK LENGTH

FRONT TRACK WIDTH (50%)

Ducks
various species

Aquatic birds with webbed feet, varying in size from the small bufflehead through mallards to pintails. Length ranges from 14 to 24 inches (35 to 60 cm). Large variety in body patterns among species. Males generally more brightly colored than females.

Mallard
Anas platyrhynchos

Track: Four toes. Toes 2 to 4, which point forward, usually register. Toe 1 points rearward and may not show. Distal webbing between toes 2, 3, and 4. Webbing concave between toes. Toes 2 and 4 tend to converge near tips. Claws are broad, blunt, and attached to toes. Feet turn in.

Trail: Walking stride of a mallard (*Anas platyrhynchos*; illustrated here) is about 4 inches (10 cm).

Scat: Pencil-sized cords, four to eight times longer than wide. Often greenish and coated with white nitrogen deposits.

Habitat: Ponds, lakes, marshes, streams, rivers, and bays.

scat
2 x 0.25 in
5 x 0.8 cm

SCAT WIDTH

Similar species: Tracks differ from geese and swans by smaller size. Differ from pelicans and cormorants by lacking webbing between toes 1 and 2. Differ from gulls by having convergent toes.

Other sign: Nests may be on the ground, in tree cavities, or on floating mats. Eggs roughly the size of chicken eggs, though there may be great variation among species.

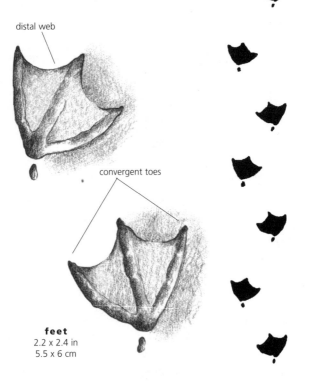

distal web

convergent toes

feet
2.2 x 2.4 in
5.5 x 6 cm

walk

FRONT TRACK LENGTH

FRONT TRACK WIDTH

Canada Goose
Branta canadensis

Medium-sized aquatic bird, average length 30 inches (75 cm). Considerable size variation among subspecies. Black head and neck, with a white chin band. Back is olive brown. Male and female similarly colored.

Track: Four toes. Toes 2 to 4, which point forward, usually register. Toe 1 points rearward and only occasionally shows. Distal webbing between toes 2, 3, and 4. Toes 2 and 4 tend to converge slightly near tips. Claws are broad, blunt, and usually attached to toes. Feet turn in.

Trail: Walking stride is about 12 inches (30 cm).

Scat: Cord, five to eight times longer than wide; as long as 3.5 inches (8.8 cm). Often greenish and coated with white nitrogenous deposits.

scat
3 x 0.4 in
7.5 x 1 cm

SCAT WIDTH

Habitat: Ponds, lakes, marshes, streams, rivers, and bays.

Similar species: Larger than most ducks and smaller than swans. Differs from pelican and cormorant by lacking webbing between toes 1 and 2. Larger than gulls, and differing from them by having convergent toes and distal webbing.

Other sign: Nests on ground, sometimes on cliff ledges, and in abandoned heron and raptor nests. Eggs larger than chicken eggs.

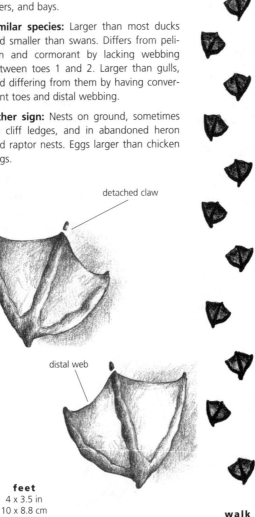

detached claw

distal web

feet
4 x 3.5 in
10 x 8.8 cm

walk

FRONT TRACK LENGTH

FRONT TRACK WIDTH

Hawks
various species

Medium-sized birds, up to 25 inches (63 cm) in length, with wingspans of 50 inches (125 cm). The red-tailed hawk (*Buteo jamaicensis*) is a highly variable, dark-colored hawk with red tail feathers. Light phase has a dark belly band.

Track: Four wide, robust toes. Toes 2 to 4 point forward. Claws are long, sharp, and not attached to the toe print.

Red-tailed hawk
Buteo jamaicensis

Trail: Walking stride of a red-tailed hawk (illustrated here) is about 12 inches (30 cm). Hops or runs after prey on the ground. Claws may drag in soft mud, creating a fringe along sides of footprint.

Scat: Semiliquid, primarily white with some brown intermixed. Unlike owls, scat is ejected with force, sometimes leaving a trail. Whitish piles and vertical streaks below nests.

cough pellets

Habitat: Woodland and open country with scattered trees.

Similar species: Smaller than eagles. Differ from owls by having three toes pointing forward. Differ from geese and swans by lacking webbing. Differ from herons and cranes by having symmetrical feet.

Other sign: Cough pellets may be 1.5 to 4 inches (3.8 to 10 cm) long.

walk

feet
4.5 x 3.2 in
11.3 x 8 cm

FRONT TRACK LENGTH

FRONT TRACK WIDTH

Eagles
two species

Large birds, averaging 35
inches (90 cm) in length,
with wingspans of 80 inches
(200 cm). Brown bodies.
Adult golden eagle
(*Aquila chrysaetos*) has
golden feathers over
head and neck. Adult bald eagle
(*Haliaeetus leucocephalus*) has white
head, neck, and tail feathers.

Bald eagle
Haliaeetus leucocephalus

Track: Four wide,
robust toes. Toes 2
to 4 point
forward.
Lacks webbing
and metatarsal
pad. Claws are
long, sharp, and not
attached to the toe print.

Trail: Walking stride about 18 inches (45 cm). Golden eagle
will run after prey on the ground.

Scat: Semiliquid, primarily white with some brown intermixed.

Habitat: Golden eagle found in hilly areas and hunts over open
country. Bald eagle usually found near lakes and rivers.

cough pellet

urine stain on rock

Similar species: Larger than hawk's track, which is less than 3 inches (7.5 cm). Differ from owls by having three toes pointing forward. Differ from geese and swans by lacking webbing. Differ from herons and cranes by having symmetrical feet.

Other sign: Cough pellets may be 5 x 1.5 inches (12.5 x 3.8 cm). Nests may be 6 feet (2 m) in diameter.

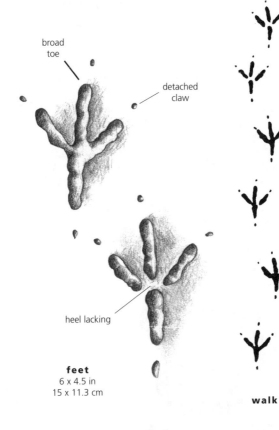

broad toe

detached claw

heel lacking

feet
6 x 4.5 in
15 x 11.3 cm

walk

FRONT TRACK LENGTH (50%)

FRONT TRACK WIDTH (50%)

Ruffed Grouse
Bonasa umbellus

Size comparable to a chicken, 17 inches (43 cm) in length. Mottled brown in color. Black feather ruffs on side of neck. Wide, multibanded tail with dark band near tip.

Track: Four toes, with toes 2 to 4 pointing forward. Toe 1, relatively short, may not show. Toes are relatively wide and lack webbing. Claws detached. In winter, a fringe of scales makes toes wider.

Trail: Walking stride is about 9 inches (23 cm). Trail is straight and feet toe in. In deep snow there can be a 4-inch (10-cm) wide trough. Look for wing marks in the snow as well as body impression under brush and evergreen trees.

Scat: Light to dark brown, sometimes with white nitrogenous covering. Content includes buds, berries, and sawdust. In winter, deposited in snow nest in large mass of fifty or so scats. May be scattered if roosting in trees.

hard form

scat
0.9 x 0.3 in
2.3 x 0.8 cm

soft form

SCAT WIDTH

Habitat: Mixed deciduous woodlands with dense understory. Prefers aspen groves.

Similar species: Tracks larger than bobwhite. Differ from other forest birds by wide, robust toe size and short toe 1. Grouse trails can be differentiated from those of other forest birds by their short stride.

Other sign: Burrow under the snow to roost. Round nests usually 5 inches (13 cm) in diameter made from leaves and brush. Dust baths in sandy areas.

walk

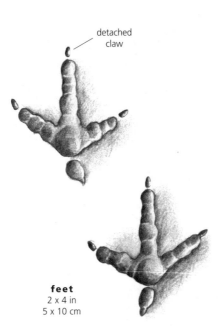

detached claw

feet
2 x 4 in
5 x 10 cm

FRONT TRACK LENGTH

FRONT TRACK WIDTH (50%)

Turkey
Meleagris gallopavo

Large, ground-dwelling bird. Males average 45 inches (113 cm) and females 35 inches (88 cm) in length. Smaller and more slender than the domesticated Thanksgiving turkey. Male has a dark brown to black body, with white stripes on flight feathers; tail feathers are tipped with brownish white. Color of female's feathers is similar but dull. Male also has red wattles, folds of skin hanging from the chin.

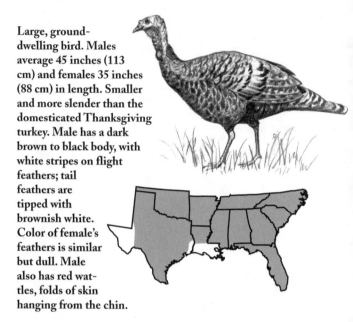

Track: Four broad, robust toes. Toes 2 to 4 face forward. Hind toe (toe 1) only occasionally registers, and then in a straight line with toe 4. Only the claw or tip of toe 1 registers. Metatarsal pad present, though it may be unattached to toes. Claws narrow and usually attached to toe.

scat
3 x 0.5 in
7.5 x 1.3 cm

tracks with scratch marks

SCAT WIDTH

Trail: Walking stride 15 inches (38 cm). Foot axis may vary, pointing into the line of travel or turning slightly out.

Scat: Solid scat is long, up to 3 inches (7.5 cm), narrow, and brown with greenish-white nitrogenous material on ends. Also produces a soft scat that piles in a shapeless mass on ground.

Habitat: Open forest, shrubland and wooded swamps, in trees with lateral branches for roosting at night.

Similar species: Differs from other birds by wide, robust toes. Tracks larger than other ground-dwelling birds. Lacks webbing of ducks and certain other aquatic birds. Separated from eagles by presence (usually) of metatarsal pad. Toes 2 and 4 point forward to a greater degree than those of crane.

Other sign: Scratches on ground where turkey digs for seeds, acorns, nuts, and insects.

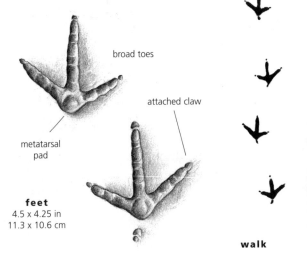

broad toes

attached claw

metatarsal pad

feet
4.5 x 4.25 in
11.3 x 10.6 cm

walk

FRONT TRACK LENGTH (50%)

FRONT TRACK WIDTH (50%)

Bobwhite
Colinus virginianus

Size comparable to a small chicken, 9 inches (23 cm) in length. Mottled reddish-brown with a short gray-colored tail. Male with white stripes on face and throat, brownish in female.

Track: Four toes, with toes 2 to 4 pointing forward. Toe 1, relatively short, may be detached or not show. Toes are relatively wide and lack webbing. Feet point forward to slightly inward.

Trail: Walking stride is about 6 inches (15 cm). Trail is straight but feet toe in.

Scat: Light to dark brown, sometimes with white nitrogenous covering.

depressions in dust from chicks

scat
1.4 x 0.2 in
3.5 x 0.5 cm

SCAT WIDTH

Habitat: Tall grasslands, brushlands, open woodlands, and cultivated fields.

Similar species: Tracks smaller than grouse. Differ from other forest birds by wide, robust toe size and short toe 1. Bobwhite trails can be differentiated from those of other forest birds by their short strides and wide straddles.

Other sign: Ground roost is a circle of shallow body depressions where birds sleep with their heads pointing out. Nest is a shallow depression under "woven" grass with a side entrance.

feet
1.75 x 1.5 in
4.4 x 3.8 cm

walk

FRONT TRACK LENGTH

FRONT TRACK WIDTH

Coot
Fulica americana

Medium-sized aquatic bird, average length 15 inches (38 cm). Slate-black body, with white beak extending into small brown forehead shield.

Track: Four toes showing, toes 2 to 4 pointing forward. Toe 1 angles inward. Toes 2, 3, and 4 have fringe of webbing with indented lobes. Long, pointed claws, especially those on toe 1, may be separated from toes.

Trail: Walking stride 10 inches (25 cm); tends to wander when walking. Foot axis parallel to line of travel.

Scat: White liquid.

Habitat: Freshwater lakes and ponds having shallow water where reeds and rushes grow.

Similar species: Differs from all other aquatic birds by the indented lobes on each toe.

Other sign: Floating nest built from cattails, sedges, and rushes, rising several inches above the water.

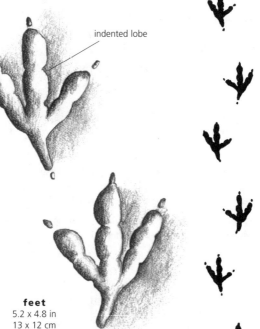

indented lobe

feet
5.2 x 4.8 in
13 x 12 cm

walk

Shorebirds
various species

Avocet
Recurvirostra americana

Many birds, such
as avocets, sand-
pipers, killdeer,
curlews, and snipes. Length
varies from 6 to 18 inches (15 to
45 cm). All have similar footprints and
differentiation is difficult.

Track: For avocets (illustrated
here) four narrow
toes, although toe 1
may not show. Toes
2 to 4 face for-
ward and are
nearly symmet-
rical around toe
3. Outer toe angle
often greater than 120
degrees. Small, proximal
webbing between toes 2, 3, and 4 may be visible, though
curlews and sandpipers have proximal webbing only between
toes 3 and 4. Avocets exhibit mesial webbing.

Trail: Shorebirds are constantly running along the water's edge.
Stride varies from 4 to 20 inches (10 to 50 cm).

Scat: Small and semiliquid. Brown, green, and white mixed.

**nest in grass
with twigs**

Habitat: Water's edge at lakes, rivers, streams, bays, and wastewater treatment plants.

Similar species: Differ from song- or perching birds by the weak showing of toe 1, which in perching birds is strong and used to grasp branches. Outer toe angle of songbirds is less than 90 degrees. Shorebirds walk or run, but most songbirds hop.

Other sign: Myriad roundish holes where beak pushed into the sand in pursuit of insects.

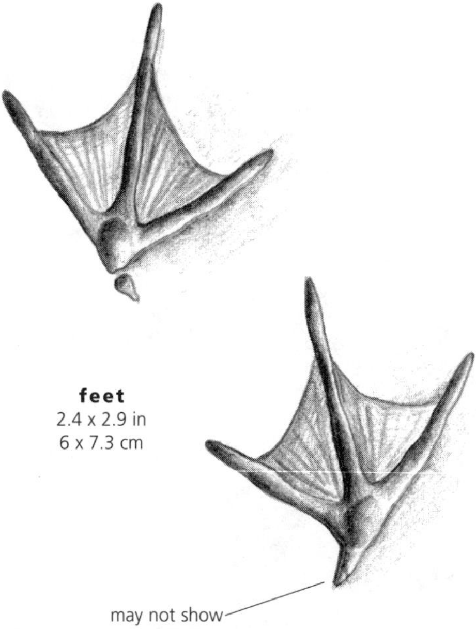

feet
2.4 x 2.9 in
6 x 7.3 cm

may not show

walk

Gulls
various species

Average length 25
inches (63 cm). Pale-
gray back, white head.
Tips of primary feathers
black. Yellow bill with red
spot; pink legs. Many species,
such as Bonaparte's,
Franklin's, Ring-billed, and
Herring gulls. Length varies
from 11 to 30 inches. White and gray-col-
ored birds with some black markings. Gregarious species of
open beaches of lakes, oceans, and rivers. Herring gull
(Larus argentatus) illustrated here.

Herring gull
Larus argentatus

Track: Four toes. Toes
2 to 4 (forward-
pointing) show.
Toe 1 may reg-
ister only
slightly or not
show at all. Web-
bing relatively straight
between toes. Toes 2 and
3 tend to diverge, especially at the tips.

Trail: Walking stride of herring gull is about 13 inches (33 cm).
Feet turn slightly inward.

Scat: Semiliquid. Primarily white, with indistinguishable contents.

cough pellet

Habitat: Along coast and on inland lakes and rivers. Nests in colonies on ground or cliffs, usually on islands. Nest is made of grass or seaweed. A scavenger, the herring gull is also found at dumps.

Similar species: Differ from ducks, swans, and geese by having divergent toes. Smaller than swans and geese. Differ from coot by having webbing between toes.

Other sign: Cough pellets containing bones, fish scales, urchin parts, and garbage. Shell fragments from mussel shells dropped onto rocks from high in the air.

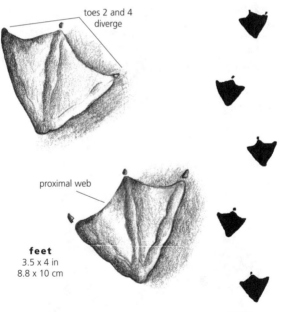

toes 2 and 4 diverge

proximal web

feet
3.5 x 4 in
8.8 x 10 cm

walk

FRONT TRACK LENGTH (50%)

FRONT TRACK WIDTH (50%)

Owls
various species

Considerable variation in length, from the saw-whet owl (*Aegolius acadicus*), 8 inches (20 cm), to the short-eared owl (*Asio flammeus*), 15 inches (38 cm), to the great horned owl (*Bubo virginianus*), 25 inches (63 cm). All species have immobile eyes offset by facial disks of feathers. Great variability in appearance among species. Typical body colors are grays, browns, and reddish browns.

Short-eared owl
Asio flammeus

Track: Four broad toes, with two paired and facing forward. Toe 4 position is not fixed and may face back or out. Lack webbing and metatarsal pads. Claws long and detached from footprint. Tracks of short-eared owl (pictured above) illustrated on facing page.

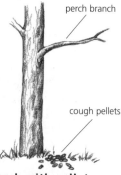

perch branch

cough pellets

cough pellet

perch with pellets

Trail: Walking stride varies considerably among species, from 3 to 10 inches (7.5 to 25 cm).

Scat: Semiliquid, primarily white.

Habitat: Forested areas. Some species, such as barn owls, will readily use human structures.

Similar species: Differ from most birds in toes 2 and 3 being paired, nearly parallel, and pointing forward. Differ from woodpeckers by toes being wide and robust, and by toes 1 and 4 being much shorter than toes 2 and 3.

Other sign: Cough pellets below a roost. Diameter of cough pellets ranges from 0.25 to 1 inch (0.6 to 2.5 cm) and is directly related to the size of the owl. Pellets are shiny and black when new but turn gray with age.

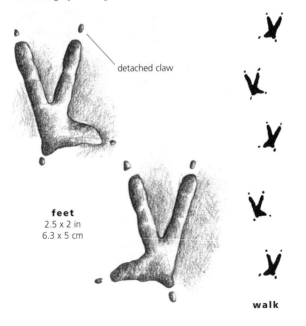

detached claw

feet
2.5 x 2 in
6.3 x 5 cm

walk

FRONT TRACK LENGTH

FRONT TRACK WIDTH

Woodpeckers
various species

Considerable variation in size. The flicker (*Colaptes auratus*) is a medium-sized woodpecker, slightly larger than the American robin, average length 12 inches (30 cm). Male has brown-barred back, black chest, white rump, red or black whisker stripe, and is yellow under wings. Female lacks whisker stripe.

Flicker
Colaptes auratus

Track: Four toes, with two parallel and pointing forward. Toes 1 and 4 point backward and are not equal in length. Strong, rigid tail feathers may show on ground.

Trail: Walking stride of the flicker (illustrated here) is about 3 inches (7.5 cm). Hopping stride is about 4 inches (10 cm).

Scat: Cord, about four or more times longer than wide. Often contains undigested parts of insects.

scat
1 x 0.25 in
2.5 x 0.6 cm

SCAT WIDTH

Habitat: Open woodlands, dense forests, and around towns.

Similar species: Differs from three-toed woodpecker by presence of toe 1. Differs from other birds its size by having two toes pointing forward.

Other sign: Excavates and nests in tree cavities. Does not add bedding material to cavity nest.

tree with beak holes

toes point forward

feet
1.75 x 0.75 in
4.4 x 1.9 cm

walk

Blue Jay
Cyanocita cristata

Small bird with blue body and white markings on wings. Prominent blue crest and black throat band. Average length about 11 inches (28 cm).

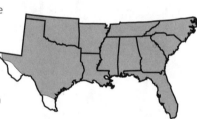

Track: Narrow track with four narrow toes, toes 2 to 4 facing forward and not widely splayed. Toe 1 as long as toes 2, 3, and 4. Toe 1 broader than other toes. Lacks webbing and metatarsal pad. Claws long, especial on toe 1.

Trail: Hopping stride is 4 to 5 inches (10 to 12.5 cm). Occasionally walks.

Scat: Semiliquid, brown to black with white intermixed.

Habitat: Woodlands, gardens, and parks.

Similar species: Differs from songbirds by larger size and relatively narrow footprint. Smaller and narrower than crows and ravens.

Other sign: Nest, on horizontal branch or tree crotch, is compact and occasionally cemented with mud.

hop

feet
2.2 x 0.5 in
5.5 x 1.3 cm

walk

FRONT TRACK LENGTH

FRONT TRACK WIDTH

Crow
Corvus brachyrhynchos

Medium-sized (17 inches / 43 cm) black bird with strong beak (smaller than raven's). Sides of tail are parallel in flight, not wedge shaped. Black feet and legs.

Track: Four toes, three facing forward. Toe 1 nearly equals toes 2, 3, and 4. Lacks webbing. Metatarsal pad present. Claws long and often detached from footprint. The footprint length of 2.5 inches (6.3 cm) includes toe 4, which adds 0.7 inch (1.8 cm).

Trail: Walking stride varies but is about 5 inches (13 cm). Crows both walk and hop and may run with a long stride.

Scat: Semiliquid brown and white, but may contain remnants of food from their omnivorous diet.

cough pellet

Habitat: Roadside, woodlands, farms, orchards, and lake and ocean shores.

Similar species: Raven track and trail is much larger than crow's. Lack the paired forward facing toes of owls. Lack long toe 1 of hawks.

Other sign: Cough pellets up to 1 x 0.4 inch (2.5 x 1.0 cm). Pellets may contain berries, seeds, nuts, insect parts, and snails, among other items of its varied diet.

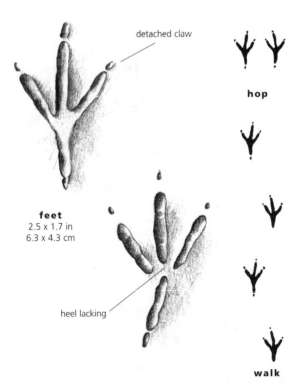

detached claw

hop

feet
2.5 x 1.7 in
6.3 x 4.3 cm

heel lacking

walk

Opossum
Didelphis marsupialis

The size of a large domestic cat, but more stout, nearly hairless, and with a round, rat-like tail. Weight varies from 8 to 14 pounds (3.5 to 6.5 kg). Face whitish, with thin, black-edged ears. Body is whitish with gray and black hairs interspersed.

Track: Five toes. Hind print is distinctive, with an opposable (like the human thumb) inside toe protruding sideways from other toes. Outside toe is slightly separated from middle three toes. Front footprint is wider than long and shows long toes that widen slightly toward the end.

Trail: Walking stride 18 inches (45 cm). Walking trail often reflects slow movement, with hind footprint registering behind the front. Trail is sloppy and footprints seldom register directly. Tail drag often shows. Walking pattern occasionally similar to that of the raccoon, where the hind footprint registers beside the front footprint.

scat shape is highly variable

scat
4 x 0.5 in
10 x 1.3 cm

SCAT WIDTH

Scat: Highly variable shape and size and lack of distinctive form reflect highly variable, omnivorous diet. Single scat may be up to 4 inches (10 cm) long.

Habitat: Prefers riparian areas, woodlands, and farmyards. Habitat is not restricted by diet, as the opossum will eat small mammals, birds, eggs, reptiles, amphibians, fish, carrion, fruit, and any garbage it can find.

Similar species: Trail may be confused with those of muskrats, woodrats, and domestic rats when a tail drag is present. However, the distinctive hind footprint and large size of the opossum footprint identify its trail.

Other sign: Dens in logs, stumps, rock crevices, and dens of other animals.

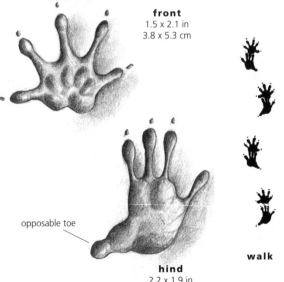

front
1.5 x 2.1 in
3.8 x 5.3 cm

opposable toe

hind
2.2 x 1.9 in
5.5 x 4.8 cm

walk

FRONT TRACK LENGTH

FRONT TRACK WIDTH

Armadillo
Dasypus novemcinctus

Size of a house cat, weighing 8 to 17 pounds (3.5 to 8 kg). Body, tail, and head are covered with a horny armor derived from the leathery skin. A few hairs are found between scales. Body color a light tan to gray. Large gray to black ears.

Track: Front tracks with four toes, hind with five. Often only the prominent inner toes, two on front, three on rear, register. Claws are prominent and broad, may appear attached, and usually dig deeply into the ground.

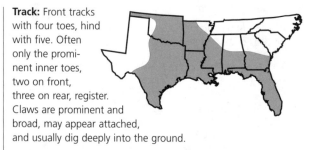

Trail: Trotting stride is about 25 inches (65 cm), walking stride around 15 inches (40 cm). Use side gaits including trots and lopes. Occasionally the belly or tail drags.

Scat: Usually elongate, but may be spherical. Usually contains insect remains and a considerable amount of dirt.

scat
2 x 0.4 in
5 x 1 cm

sign

SCAT WIDTH

Habitat: Usually dry, sandy areas, including brush, woodlands, and chaparral. Seem to additionally prefer rocky areas and cliffs.

Similar species: Easily separated from other mammals by prominent claws and odd numbers of toes in tracks.

Other sign: Digs out ant mounds and disturbs ground litter as it roots for insects. Digs long dwelling burrows that are around 8 inches (20 cm) in diameter. Pulls vegetation into the burrows to form a nest.

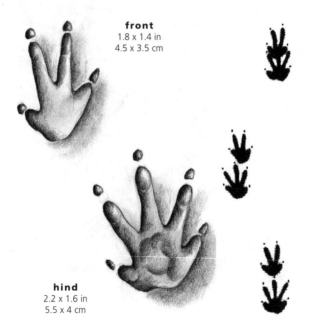

front
1.8 x 1.4 in
4.5 x 3.5 cm

hind
2.2 x 1.6 in
5.5 x 4 cm

walk

FRONT TRACK LENGTH

FRONT TRACK WIDTH

Shrews
various species

Smaller than mice, less than 0.25 ounce (7 g). Long, pointed nose. Minute eyes and ears. Color brown to black, with gray to white belly. Eat mostly insects. The masked shrew (*Sorex cinereus*) illustrated here.

Masked shrew
Sorex cinereus

Track: Five slender toes are present on front and hind feet. In clear prints, four interdigital and two proximal pads may be seen.

Trail: Hopping stride of the masked shrew is seldom more than 2 inches (5 cm). The group of tracks is less than 1 inch (2.5 cm) long. Seldom is the stride more than three times the group.

Scat: Usually small pellets with tapered ends.

Habitat: Found everywhere from grasslands to forests. Look for tracks in wet, fine mud of riparian areas or in snow along logs or

scat
0.2 x 0.1 in
0.5 x 0.3 cm

tapered ends

insect remains

SCAT WIDTH

the edges of buildings. Woodpiles and leaf litter make good homes.

Similar species: Differ from mice and voles by having five toes on front foot.

Other sign: After eating, leave body parts from insects they have killed. Often burrow just below the surface of the snow, opening tunnels that partially collapse and expose their route. Trails in the snow radiate from holes like spokes of a wheel.

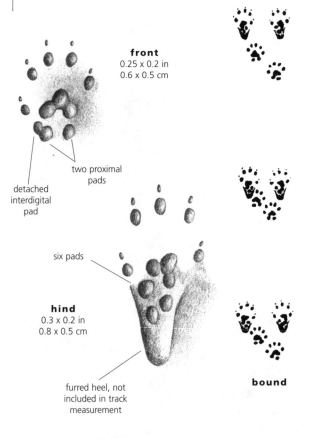

front
0.25 x 0.2 in
0.6 x 0.5 cm

two proximal pads

detached interdigital pad

six pads

hind
0.3 x 0.2 in
0.8 x 0.5 cm

furred heel, not included in track measurement

bound

FRONT TRACK LENGTH

FRONT TRACK WIDTH

Red Fox
Vulpes vulpes

Border collie–sized, 6
to 15 pounds (3 to 7
kg). Reddish yellow,
with black stockings
and a white tip on the tail.
Regional color phases
include silver, black, cross,
and bluish gray. Long, pointed ears and elongate, pointed
muzzle.

Track: Claws promi-
nent. One lobe on
the leading
edge of the
interdigital pad.
Inside toe slightly
larger than outside.
A ridge of callus present
across interdigital pad, but
difficult to detect on hind footprint. Front foot larger than hind.

Trail: Trotting stride averages 32 inches (80 cm). Typically uses a
trotting gait and, occasionally, a 2 x 2 trot with body turned to the
side. Walks more than coyote, especially in shrubs.

Scat: Often has tapered tail. Composition varies. Mouse or rabbit
fur, berries, and insects are common. Bird feathers and plant
remains often present.

scat
2 x 0.6 in
5 x 1.5 cm

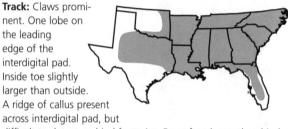

log

SCAT WIDTH

Habitat: Found in a variety of habitats from brush to croplands to mixed hard- and softwood forest. Prefers edges, where hunting for small mammals is good. Also found in urban areas, where cover is available during the daytime. Not found in dense forests.

Similar species: Differs from other canids by having a ridge of callus on the interdigital pad. Track tends to be larger than gray fox, and usually shows claws. Differs from bobcat in having only one lobe on the interdigital pad and claws (usually) showing.

Other sign: Multiple dens are used each season. Often digs own den. A given den may be used for several years. Look for small bones around den entrance. Scat has a diagnostic musky odor, produced by a musk gland on the top of the tail. Learn to identify this unique foxy odor. Foxes tightrope-walk on narrow logs. May take over woodchuck dens.

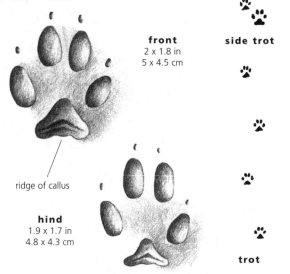

side trot

front
2 x 1.8 in
5 x 4.5 cm

ridge of callus

hind
1.9 x 1.7 in
4.8 x 4.3 cm

trot

FRONT TRACK LENGTH

FRONT TRACK WIDTH

Gray Fox
Urocyon cinereoargenteus

Smaller than a border collie, 8 to 11 pounds (4 to 5 kg). Body color is pepper-and-salt. A black stripe runs down the back and upper side of tail. Sides are reddish. Tip of tail is black. Long, pointed ears and elongate, pointed muzzle.

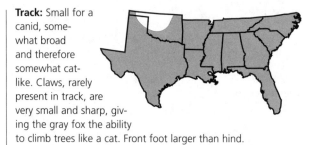

Track: Small for a canid, somewhat broad and therefore somewhat cat-like. Claws, rarely present in track, are very small and sharp, giving the gray fox the ability to climb trees like a cat. Front foot larger than hind.

Trail: Generally a trot. Trotting stride averages 24 inches (60 cm). Walks more than coyote.

Scat: Often has tapered tail. Composition varies, as the gray fox is opportunistic when feeding. Rabbit fur is most common, followed by fur of other small mammals, berries, and insects. Plant remains are often present.

scat
2 x 0.6 in
5 x 1.5 cm

SCAT WIDTH

Habitat: Prefers a mixture of fields and woods. More often found in woodlands than is red fox. Early stage woodlands are preferred, with considerable activity in riparian habitats.

Similar species: Smaller than coyote. Lacks the ridge of callus on the interdigital pad of the red fox. Differs from coyote in that claws often do not show.

Other sign: Seldom digs dens, but makes use of woodpiles, rock outcrops, hollow trees, and brushpiles. Look for small bones around den entrances.

side trot

front
1.8 x 1.6 in
4.5 x 4 cm

climbing tree

no callus ridge

hind
1.7 x 1.6 in
4.3 x 4 cm

trot

FRONT TRACK LENGTH

FRONT TRACK WIDTH

Coyote
Canis latrans

Collie-sized canid, 20 to 30 pounds (9 to 13.5 kg). Male larger than female. Large males can exceed 35 pounds. Color varies from completely gray to tan to rust. Long, pointed ears and long, narrow muzzle.

Track: Claws usually present. One lobe on the leading edge of the interdigital pad. Inside toe slightly larger than outside. Front foot larger than hind.

Trail: Trotting stride averages 41 inches (94 cm). Often uses a trot with body turned to the side, leaving a 2 x 2 track pattern. Often lopes, leaving a C-shaped pattern.

Scat: Varies from pure black animal protein to mostly hair with some bones. Tips tapered into long tails.

scat
3 x 0.75 in
7.5 x 1.88 cm

scratch marks near scat pile

SCAT WIDTH

Habitat: An animal of the open brush country, the coyote digs its den on exposed hilltops or ridges with a view of surrounding area. Where persecuted, may den in a more secluded location.

Similar species: Track may overlap in size with red fox, but lacks callus ridge of red fox. Track larger than gray fox, and usually shows claws. Differs from bobcat by showing claws and by having one lobe on leading edge of interdigital pad.

Other sign: Marks territory with urine and scat piles. Scat pile locations may be used repeatedly. Uses feet to scratch near scat piles, spreading odor from scat and foot glands to identify territory.

lope

front
2.75 x 2.5 in
6.9 x 6.3 cm

hind
2.5 x 2.2 in
6.3 x 5.5 cm

side trot

FRONT TRACK LENGTH

FRONT TRACK WIDTH

Ocelot
Felis pardalis

Collie-sized, weighing up to 35 pounds (16 kg). More slender than a bobcat. Body color is gray, buff, or cinnamon with black-rimmed brown markings ranging in shape from spots on body to stripes on neck. Underside white with black markings. Long tail marked with black stripes or rings.

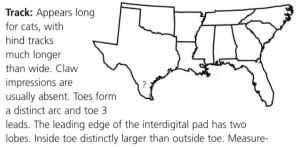

Track: Appears long for cats, with hind tracks much longer than wide. Claw impressions are usually absent. Toes form a distinct arc and toe 3 leads. The leading edge of the interdigital pad has two lobes. Inside toe distinctly larger than outside toe. Measurements from five ocelots from Texas.

Trail: Trotting stride is about 40 inches (100 cm).

Scat: Tends to be constricted and, if dry, separates at constrictions into segments. Dry scat falls apart. Ends usually blunt. Scat from

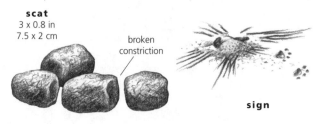

scat
3 x 0.8 in
7.5 x 2 cm

broken constriction

sign

a fresh kill may form a uniform-diameter cord. Defecates at latrines, where feces accumulate.

Habitat: Seldom far from trees or dense cover. In Texas, found in dense, thorny chaparral of mesquite and acacia.

Similar species: Smaller than lion. Definitive characteristics are not available to separate ocelot tracks from bobcat. However, tracks are probably longer. Differ from those of fox by presence of two lobes on the anterior edge of the interdigital pad.

Other sign: Probably scent marks with urine and scat. Scrapes dirt over scat. Scratches trees and fence posts.

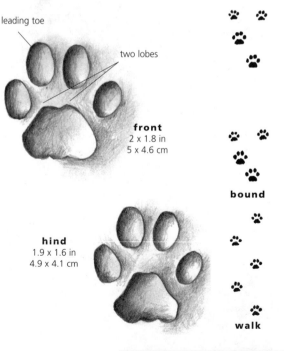

walk

**vertical leap
from hind
feet**

leading toe

two lobes

front
2 x 1.8 in
5 x 4.6 cm

hind
1.9 x 1.6 in
4.9 x 4.1 cm

bound

walk

FRONT TRACK LENGTH

FRONT TRACK WIDTH

Bobcat
Felis rufus

Size of a collie, weighing 13 to 35 pounds (6 to 16 kg). Males larger than females. Overall color reddish to yellowish brown, with dark spots or streaks and whitish underside. Ears have tufts at tips. Back of ears and top of tail tip black. Tail is short or bobbed, about 4 inches (10 cm) long.

Track: Front track is round or wider than long. Hind track may be longer than wide. Claw impressions are usually absent. Toes form a slight arc and toe 3 leads. The leading edge of the interdigital pad has two lobes. Inside toe distinctly larger than outside toe.

Trail: Walking stride is about 20 inches (50 cm). Usually walks, but bounds with hind feet placed side by side when chasing prey. Winter trails often show random vertical leaps, perhaps signaling that the bobcat has jumped after a flying bird.

Scat: Tends to be constricted and, if dry, separates at constrictions into segments. Ends usually blunt. Dry scat falls apart. Scat from a fresh kill may form a cord of uniform diameter.

broken constriction

scat
3 x 0.8 in
7.5 x 2 cm

SCAT WIDTH

Habitat: Prefers dense cover of swamps and forests, especially with rocky ledges. Open agricultural land is not used. Rock piles, caves, and high rocky ledges are important for bearing young.

Similar species: Differs from coyote and other canids by lacking claws, having two lobes on the leading edge of the interdigital pad, and having toe 3 leading. Substantially smaller than lion. Definitive characteristics are not available to separate ocelot tracks from bobcat. However, tracks are probably longer.

Other sign: Scent marks made by urine, scat, and anal glands. Scrapes dirt or snow over urine and scat. Scratches from rubbing glands are apparent on snow. Caches food by burying.

walk

vertical leap from hind feet

bound

walk

leading toe

two lobes

front
2 x 2.1 in
5 x 5.5 cm

claw marks on tree

hind
2.1 x 1.9 in
5.3 x 4.8 cm

FRONT TRACK LENGTH

FRONT TRACK WIDTH

Mountain Lion
Puma concolor

Larger than a German shepherd, with male about 145 pounds (66 kg) and female about 120 pounds (54 kg). Color gray to red, often called tawny, with whitish underside. Back of ears and tip of tail black to brown. Tail is more than half the length of the body. Also called cougar or puma. Scattered reports in east where they may be reestablishing, track verification needed—photos or casts.

Track: Track diameter of a baseball. Front track round or wider than long, and hind track longer than wide. Claw impressions are usually absent. Toes form a slight arc and toe 3 leads. Leading edge of the interdigital pad has two lobes. Inside toe distinctly larger.

Trail: Walking stride is about 36 inches (90 cm). Usually walks, but bounds with hind feet placed side by side when chasing prey.

Scat: Scat from a fresh kill may form a cord of uniform diameter with very slight constrictions; ends usually blunt. As the carcass a lion is feeding on dries out, the lion's scat tends to develop constrictions, eventually falling apart when diet becomes very dry.

scat
4 x 1.25 in
10 x 3.1 cm

SCAT WIDTH

Habitat: Habitat is that of its main prey, deer. Open woodlands with rock ledges and grass (for deer) preferred. Often found in riparian zones with trees.

Similar species: Differs from bear by having only four toes and large toe inside. Larger than other cats.

Other sign: Often buries scat by scraping dirt over it with front feet. Scraped ground material may conceal food caches. Male will rake up basketball-sized patches of brush and urinate on them to mark home range.

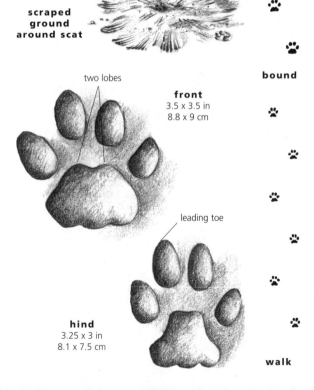

scraped ground around scat

bound

two lobes

front
3.5 x 3.5 in
8.8 x 9 cm

leading toe

hind
3.25 x 3 in
8.1 x 7.5 cm

walk

FRONT TRACK LENGTH

FRONT TRACK WIDTH

Black Bear
Ursus americanus

Calf-sized bear, female averaging 120 pounds (54 kg) and male about 300 pounds (135 kg). Coastal North Carolina male black bear can average over 400 pounds. Male grows faster and obtains larger size than female. Color varies from black to brown to blond to red.

Track: Claws on front foot, seldom longer than toes, are usually present. Little toe is set back from rest of toes. Hind print has a large, humanlike heel. Outside toe is larger than others.

Trail: Walking stride 35 to 40 inches (88 to 100 cm). Usually ambles, a fast walk where the hind foot oversteps the front. Gait is pigeon-toed. Lopes in a C-shaped pattern or a side gallop.

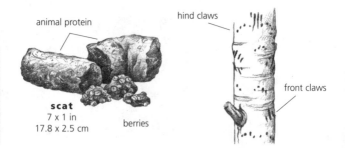

animal protein

scat
7 x 1 in
17.8 x 2.5 cm

berries

hind claws

front claws

SCAT WIDTH

Scat: Normally contains vegetation and is sweet-smelling. When feeding on carcasses, scat varies from black to brown, with mostly hair and some bones. Ants often found in scat. Tips have a short taper or are blunt.

Habitat: Forest, seldom venturing far into wide openings. Thick understory vegetation and abundant food sources are critical.

Similar species: Differs from lion by presence of five toes.

Other sign: Claws trees, rips open logs, digs into ant piles, and turns over rocks and scat as it looks for insects.

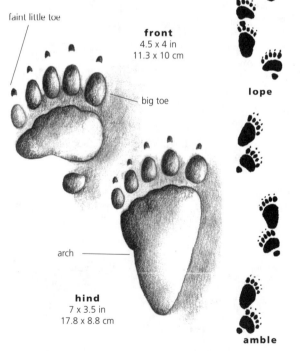

faint little toe

front
4.5 x 4 in
11.3 x 10 cm

big toe

arch

hind
7 x 3.5 in
17.8 x 8.8 cm

side lope

lope

amble

FRONT TRACK LENGTH (50%)

FRONT TRACK WIDTH (50%)

Ringtail
Bassariscus astutus

Small, rat-sized, with a bushy tail as long as its body.
Males average 1.5 to 2.5 pounds (0.7 to 1.1 kg), with
females slightly smaller. Pointed face, large
eyes and ears. Tan to gray overall, with
some black hairs. Tail has
black bands alternating with
white to a black tip.

Track: Five toes,
round and somewhat
bulbous, with
an extra proxi-
mal pad show-
ing in the front
print. Claws are
semi-retractile and
may not show.

Trail: Bounding stride is 12 to 16 inches (30 to 40 cm).
Uses a relatively slow bound or lope much of the time.

Scat: Usually composed of plant material, but occasionally black
animal protein scats are found. Insects and fruits are often present.

Habitat: Found in a variety of habitats from riparian to desert to
open woodland to evergreen forest. Rest sites and dens are

scat
2 x 0.4 in
5 x 1 cm

**chewed cactus on
cliff runway**

SCAT WIDTH

located in rocks, burrows, brushpiles, and hollow limbs. Not averse to using buildings for nests and dens.

Similar species: Differs from domestic cats, bobcats, and small foxes by having five toes and an extra proximal pad.

Other sign: Runways at the bases of cliffs are used repeatedly, and trails often lead to a single rock crevice where it dens.

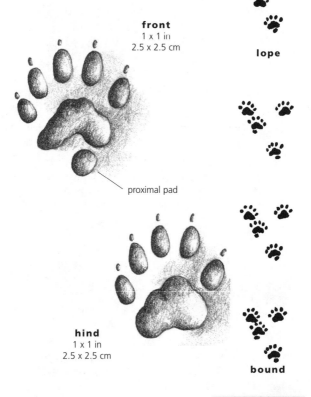

front
1 x 1 in
2.5 x 2.5 cm

lope

proximal pad

hind
1 x 1 in
2.5 x 2.5 cm

bound

FRONT TRACK LENGTH

FRONT TRACK WIDTH

Raccoon
Procyon lotor

Stocky, smaller than a collie, with broad head and bushy tail. Male averages 18 pounds (8 kg) and female 16 pounds (7 kg). Gray to black overall, with black rings on the tail and a black mask on a white face.

Track: Five slender toes, slightly bulbous on the ends. Feet resemble small human hands and feet. Hind foot has a long, naked heel.

Trail: Walking stride averages 27 inches (68 cm). Roll of hips during walk causes hind foot to register beside the opposite front print. C-shaped gallop is common.

Scat: Highly variable, but often black, even-diameter cord with blunt ends. Often contains crayfish or fruit. Deposited singly or in dung heaps containing scat from perhaps several individuals. **May**

scat
3 x 0.75 in
7.5 x 1.9 cm

sign left while fishing for crayfish

SCAT WIDTH

carry a parasite that is fatal to humans. Do not smell scat, and wash hands after touching.

Habitat: River and stream drainages are prime habitats, but storm drains in cities may also provide refuge. Woodpiles in and around towns.

Similar species: Differs from bear in having slender toes. Differs from river otter by lack of webbing. Larger than mink.

Other sign: Digs holes in stream banks to get at crayfish. Leaves piles of crayfish skeletons and claws. Digs for worms in lawns.

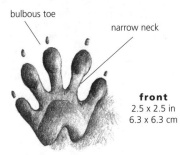

bulbous toe

narrow neck

front
2.5 x 2.5 in
6.3 x 6.3 cm

hind
4 x 2.3 in
10 x 5.8 cm

gallop

walk

FRONT TRACK LENGTH

FRONT TRACK WIDTH

Long-tailed Weasel
Mustela frenata

The size of a foot-
long hotdog.
Pointed, flat skull
with small ears. Males
weigh about 1 pound (0.45
kg). Males up to twice as
large as females. Overall color is brown, with a white belly.
In winter, northern individuals turn entirely white. Hairy,
slender tail.

Track: Wide track.
Five toes, in 1-3-1
grouping. Little
toe, on inside of
foot, often does
not register. Inter-
digital pad chevron-
shaped. Heel seldom
shows. Difficult to distinguish among species.

Trail: Galloping stride varies from 8 to 30 inches (20 to 75 cm). Side-by-side tracks, when examined closely, show one track slightly in front of the other—a gallop. In snow, a drag mark may be found between front and hind prints, sometimes forming a dumbbell shape.

Scat: Long, slender cord, usually with black, toothpaste-like animal protein or hair. Cord tends to fold back on itself. Tapered at both ends.

folded back ———

scat
1.5 x 0.1 in
3.5 x 0.3 cm

SCAT WIDTH

tail

Habitat: Prefer dense, low ground cover to open areas. Found in habitats where their prey, rodents, occur in high densities. Trails often lead from one rodent den to another. Travel in snow and ground burrows of other mammals.

Similar species: Differ from other mustelids by their smaller size and the drag mark commonly located between twin track patterns in the snow.

Other sign: Routes seldom follow a straight line, often having many sharp turns. Scat often deposited on raised objects.

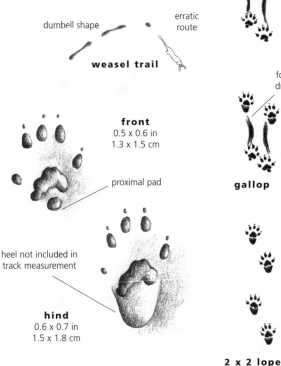

dumbbell shape

erratic route

weasel trail

front
0.5 x 0.6 in
1.3 x 1.5 cm

proximal pad

heel not included in track measurement

hind
0.6 x 0.7 in
1.5 x 1.8 cm

foot drag

gallop

2 x 2 lope

FRONT TRACK LENGTH

FRONT TRACK WIDTH

Badger
Taxidea taxus

Border collie–sized, with flat body, long hair, and long, shovel-like claws, about 18 pounds (8 kg). Male 25 percent larger than female. Color varies from silver-gray to yellowish brown on back. Belly white. Feet are black or dark brown. White stripe down nose with black markings on sides of face. Short tail.

Track: Diameter of a golf ball, with long front claws, nearly as long as rest of footprint. Five toes, in 1-3-1 grouping. Little toe, on the inside of foot, some-times does not register. Inter-digital pad chevron shaped. Proximal pad often shows. Front footprint larger than hind.

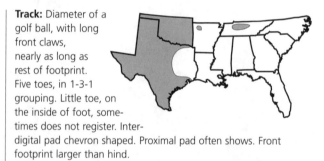

Trail: Walking stride averages 14 inches (35 cm). Walking is most common, but trotting, with a stride of 29 inches (73 cm), occurs frequently.

scat
3 x 0.8 in
7.5 x 2 cm

blunt ends

hole with dirt mound

SCAT WIDTH

Scat: Seldom found because deposited below ground in burrows. Similar to, but smaller than, coyote scat, without tapered ends.

Habitat: Open grasslands preferred. Areas with large populations of prey, which includes ground squirrels and prairie dogs.

Similar species: Differs from all other species by long claws on front foot and disproportionately small hind foot.

Other sign: Fresh excavations of large amounts of dirt from burrowing rodent holes indicates hunting activity, especially if excavated material includes large clods or rocks. Freshly widened burrow entrances may have a slightly elliptical shape. The presence of coyote and badger tracks together indicates cooperative hunting.

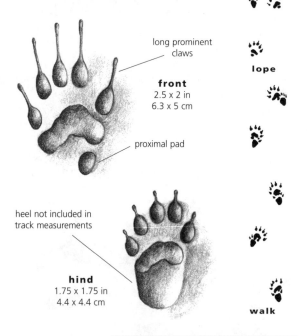

long prominent claws

front
2.5 x 2 in
6.3 x 5 cm

proximal pad

heel not included in track measurements

hind
1.75 x 1.75 in
4.4 x 4.4 cm

lope

walk

FRONT TRACK LENGTH

FRONT TRACK WIDTH

Mink
Mustela vison

Size of a small domestic cat, but slender, 1.5 to 3.5 pounds (0.7 to 1.5 kg). Male 10 percent larger than female. Pointed, flat skull with small ears. Overall color is dark brown, with white spots on chin and chest. Hairy, slender tail. Webbing occurs between the toes.

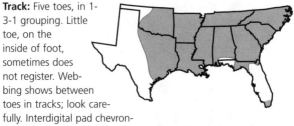

Track: Five toes, in 1-3-1 grouping. Little toe, on the inside of foot, sometimes does not register. Webbing shows between toes in tracks; look carefully. Interdigital pad chevron-shaped. Proximal pad may show in front footprint. Heel seldom shows.

Trail: Bounding stride averages 14 inches (35 cm). Bounds more than weasels, but a gallop, averaging 20 inches (50 cm), is also common.

Scat: Long, slender cord, usually tending to fold back on itself. Black or brown in color, occasionally with hair. Tapered at both

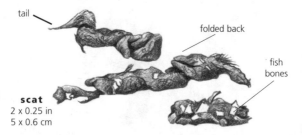

tail

folded back

fish bones

scat
2 x 0.25 in
5 x 0.6 cm

SCAT WIDTH

ends. Often contains remains of fish or cray-fish. May be oily and smell fishy. Fish oil keeps scat composed of fish scales from falling apart until oil evaporates, then scales scatter on the ground.

Habitat: River- and streambanks. Seldom far from water.

Similar species: Differs from other small mustelids by having more webbing between toes. Larger than weasels. Use of aquatic habitat is an important clue for separation from marten. Tracks and trail much smaller than otter's.

Other sign: Mink make "post offices," repeated scat deposits on logs exposed above water's edge. Strong, musky, almost skunk-like odor from anal scent glands.

fast walk

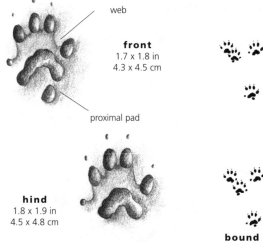

web

front
1.7 x 1.8 in
4.3 x 4.5 cm

proximal pad

hind
1.8 x 1.9 in
4.5 x 4.8 cm

bound

FRONT TRACK LENGTH

FRONT TRACK WIDTH

River Otter
Lutra canadensis

Body and tail form a 4-foot-long cylinder that tapers to a hairy, pointed tail. Weight varies from 10 to 30 pounds (5 to 14 kg). Male slightly larger than female. Overall color a rich, dark brown, with silver-brown belly. Webbed toes on front and hind feet.

Track: Large webbed foot is diagnostic, but look closely because webbing may be difficult to see. Hind foot is very wide. Five toes, in 1-3-1 grouping. Little toe, on the inside of foot, sometimes does not register. Interdigital pad chevron shaped. Proximal pad often shows. Hairless heel on hind foot.

Trail: Walking stride averages 19 inches (48 cm). Loping stride averages 32 inches (80 cm). Loping gait patterns are usually turned to the side.

Scat: Usually contains fish remains, including scales and vertebrae. The texture is oily and the smell fishy. Fish oil keeps scat composed of fish scales from falling apart. Scat decomposes as oil evaporates, eventually falling into a pile of scales.

fish parts

scat
5 x 1 in
12.5 x 2.5 cm

SCAT WIDTH

Habitat: River- and streambeds. Lives and nests in bank burrows, but may also nest in logjams. In spring, travels overland, often several miles from water sources.

Similar species: Differs from other species by webbing and large, wide hind foot.

Other sign: Loose dirt banks show where otters have rolled to dry off. Rolls around tufts of grass, twisting them into scent posts. Travels by sliding down banks and along level snow and over ice-covered lakes.

tail drag

side lope

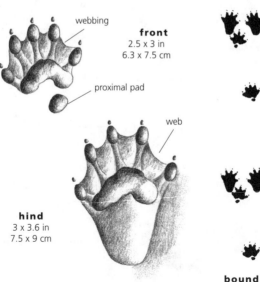

webbing

front
2.5 x 3 in
6.3 x 7.5 cm

proximal pad

web

hind
3 x 3.6 in
7.5 x 9 cm

bound

FRONT TRACK LENGTH

FRONT TRACK WIDTH

Spotted Skunk
Spilogale putorius

Black and white, size of small domestic cat. Male weighs 1 to 2 pounds (0.5 to 0.9 kg), female 0.5 to 1.25 pounds (0.25 to 0.6 kg). Distinctive pattern of white spot on forehead, a spot by each ear, four white stripes along each side, and a white tip on tail. Spots and stripes highly variable.

Track: Size of a quarter, with longer claws on front footprint. Five toes, though 1-3-1 grouping is difficult to identify. Little toe, on the inside of foot, may not register.

Clear front and hind prints on a hard surface may show a total of six hairless interdigital and proximal pads. Plantigrade heel on hind foot.

Trail: Loping stride is about 12 inches (30 cm). Short bounds are very common. Often rambles as it walks, leaving a confused trail with most front and hind prints registering separately.

scat
1.5 x 0.25 in
3.8 x 0.6 cm

blunt

insect remains

SCAT WIDTH

Scat: Cylindrical, with blunt ends. Lacks the long taper and tendency to fold back on itself of other mustelid scat. May include mouse fur, bird feathers, insects, and carrion.

Habitat: Brush, chaparral, and open woodlands, especially along streams and in boulder areas.

Similar species: Distinguished from striped skunk by smaller track size and multiple foot pads.

Other sign: Nests in burrows beneath rock- and woodpiles or under buildings.

lope

front
0.9 x 1 in
2.3 x 2.5 cm

faint pad

heel not included in
track measurement

hind
1.25 x 0.9 in
3.1 x 2.3 cm

side lope

Striped Skunk
Mephitis mephitis

Black-and-white mustelid, size of a domestic cat, with triangular head. Weight varies from 4 to 10 pounds (2 to 5 kg). Male is slightly larger than female. Flat, wide, bushy tail with white hair on top. Long, curved claws for digging.

Track: Half dollar-sized, with long front claws. Hind track looks like a little human footprint. Five toes, in 1-3-1 grouping. Little toe, on the inside of foot, some-times does not register. Interdigital pad chevron-shaped. Proximal pad often shows. Hairless heel on hind foot.

Trail: Walking stride averages 12 inches (30 cm). Meanders and stops often when walking, leaving extra footprints in trail. Lope may be turned to the side or straight forward.

Scat: Cylindrical with blunt ends. Lacks the long taper and tendency to fold back on itself of other mustelid scat. May be composed entirely of insect parts.

scat
5 x 0.75 in
12.5 x 1.9 cm

blunt

fanged puncture

chewed eggs

Habitat: Not habitat-specific. Lives where burrows, cavities, or tunnels are present, including in and around buildings. Presence of insects and small mammals is critical to habitat selection.

Similar species: Differs from other species by having long, wide claws on the front foot. Smaller than badger, with front and hind feet similar in size.

Other sign: Smell of skunk musk identifies nests and burrows. Tears apart nests of small mammals. Bird eggs show four fang punctures around larger hole in shell.

long, wide
claws

insect remains

front
1.5 x 1.25 in
3.8 x 3.1 cm

proximal pad

1 x 2 x 1 lope

hind
1.9 x 1.4 in
4.8 x 3.5 cm

side lope

FRONT TRACK LENGTH

FRONT TRACK WIDTH

Cottontail Rabbit
Sylvilagus species

Small rabbit with large ears and feet, but small white tail. Averages about 3 pounds (1.4 kg). Color pepper-and-salt or gray and white. Eastern cottontail (*S. floridanus*) illustrated here. Several species of cottontail are found in the region. The tracks of these species are indistinguishable from one another.

Eastern cottontail
Sylvilagus floridanus

Track: Toes asymmetrical around foot axis. Track indistinct because the foot is completely haired and lacks pads. Occasionally claws will register; these may be the only sign of a hopping rabbit. Hind footprint about two and a half times longer than front.

Trail: Hopping stride is about 3 feet (90 cm). Most of the time rabbits hop, but walking patterns will occasionally be observed.

Scat: Dry scat is a slightly flattened sphere. Produces a black, semiliquid scat that is usually reingested to utilize remaining nutrients.

scat
0.2 in
0.5 cm

chewed branch and bud

SCAT WIDTH

Habitat: Found wherever there is grass for food and suitable cover, including brushpiles, herbaceous and shrubby vegetation, and grasslands. May use dens of other animals for escape cover.

Similar species: Differs from snowshoe hare by having shorter heels and smaller overall size.

Other sign: Sharp incisors cleanly cut herbaceous vegetation at the height of a sitting rabbit 4 to 8 inches (10 to 20 cm). Look for tips of branches with young sprouts chewed off. The cottontail's bed, known as a form, is a shallow depression in earth, grass, or snow.

walk

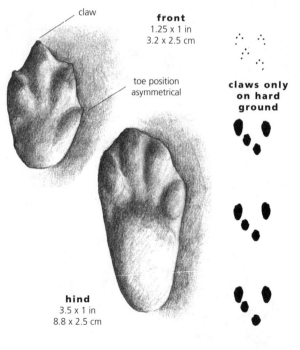

claw

front
1.25 x 1 in
3.2 x 2.5 cm

toe position
asymmetrical

**claws only
on hard
ground**

hind
3.5 x 1 in
8.8 x 2.5 cm

hop

FRONT TRACK LENGTH

FRONT TRACK WIDTH

Black-tailed Jackrabbit
Lepus californicus

Large, slender hare with long
(6 in/15 cm) ears and large
feet. Weighs 3 to 7
pounds (1.4 to 3.2 kg).
Body color is brownish
gray. Tips of ears, top
of tail, and rump are black.

Track: Toes asymmetrical
around foot axis. Track indistinct because the
foot is completely
haired and lacks
pads. Claws
occasionally
register; on
hard ground, they
may be the only sign
of a footprint. Hind footprint about three times
longer than front. Footprints of white-tailed jackrabbit are about
10 percent longer.

Trail: Galloping stride may reach 10 feet (3 m). Tends to gallop
rather than bound.

scat
0.3 in
0.8 cm

**sharp cut
grass**

SCAT WIDTH

Scat: Dry scat is a slightly flattened sphere. Produces a black, semiliquid scat that is usually reingested to utilize remaining nutrients.

Habitat: Sparsely vegetated open areas of the desert and plains.

Similar species: Hind track differs from cottontail by greater length.

Other sign: Sharp incisors cleanly cut herbaceous vegetation at the height of a sitting rabbit, 4 to 6 inches (10 to 15 cm). The jackrabbit's nest, known as a *form*, is a shallow depression, usually located under protective cover.

toe position asymmetrical

front
1.5 x 1.2 in
3.8 x 3 cm

hind
up to 4.8 x 1.4 in
up to 12 x 3.5 cm

gallop

FRONT TRACK LENGTH

FRONT TRACK WIDTH

Ground Squirrels
Spermophilus species

Size of a small rat, 0.25 to 0.5 pound (110 to 220 g). White belly. Thirteen-lined ground squirrel (*S. tridecemlineatus*) illustrated here. Body is light to dark brown with thirteen white stripes or rows of spots.

Thirteen-lined ground squirrel
Spermophilus tridecemlineatus

Track: Front print has four toes, with 1-2-1 grouping. Hind has five toes, with 1-3-1 grouping. Toes relatively slender. Front footprint size of a quarter. Hind heel is hairless and may register clearly in track. Long claws may show, especially in front tracks.

Trail: Bounding stride averages 20 inches (44 cm). Uses a half bound, characteristic of its terrestrial lifestyle.

Scat: Small, usually unconnected ovals.

scat
0.1 in
0.3 cm

SCAT WIDTH

burrow entrance

Habitat: Found in grassy areas, including pastures, lawns of cemeteries, and golf courses.

Similar species: Claws longer and feet smaller than those of tree squirrels. Smaller than woodchucks.

Other sign: Extensive burrow systems with a labyrinth of entranceways and galleries. Entrances are well hidden in vegetation and seldom have dirt at the entrances.

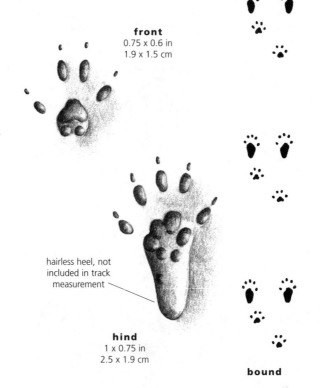

front
0.75 x 0.6 in
1.9 x 1.5 cm

hairless heel, not included in track measurement

hind
1 x 0.75 in
2.5 x 1.9 cm

bound

FRONT TRACK LENGTH

FRONT TRACK WIDTH

Woodchuck
Marmota monax

Size of a domestic cat, 5 to 10 pounds (2.2 to 4.5 kg). Ears and head are short and broad. Tail about one-third body length. Color frosted brown to yellowish brown on back, but paler on belly, dark feet.

Track: Front foot size of a silver dollar, with four toes in 1-2-1 grouping. Five toes on hind foot, 1-3-1 grouping. Toes relatively slender. Four joined interdigital and two proximal pads on front footprint and four joined interdigital pads on hind foot. Heel is hairless.

Trail: Half-bound stride varies from 15 to 40 inches (33 to 88 cm). A ground dweller, the woodchuck uses a half-bound. Walking stride is 18 inches (40 cm).

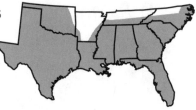

Scat: Rare to find because it is deposited in latrines within tunnel systems. Wide variety of forms, from oval pellets to long cords, all of which may be tightly stuck together. Sometimes lacks defined shape, being dark and runny when deposited.

Habitat: Open or brushy areas, especially around rocky ravines and cultivated fields.

scat
0.25 to 0.5 in diameter
0.6 to 1.3 cm

SCAT WIDTH

Similar species: Largest of the squirrels, its track dwarfs other ground squirrels. Track left when drinking at a stream may be distinguished from beaver's by lack of webbing and by having only four toes on front prints.

Other sign: Extensive tunnel system with two or more round-oval openings 5 to 7 inches (12.5 to 15 cm) in diameter. While some openings may have large mounds of dirt, others, excavated to the inside, may not have a mound and may be more concealed. Fresh dirt indicates occupancy; if height of burrow exceeds 8 inches (18 cm), it may have been taken over by red fox.

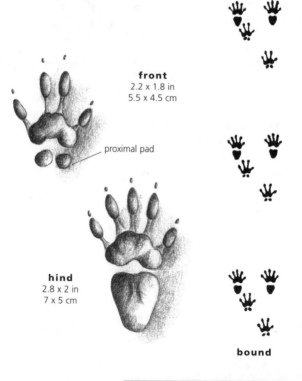

front
2.2 x 1.8 in
5.5 x 4.5 cm

proximal pad

hind
2.8 x 2 in
7 x 5 cm

bound

FRONT TRACK LENGTH

FRONT TRACK WIDTH

Chipmunk
Tamias striatus

Slightly larger than a large mouse, up to 3 ounces (80 g). Reddish fur, with white stripes bordered by black stripes along the sides of the face and body. Haired tail.

Track: Front foot size of a nickel, with four toes in 1-2-1 grouping. Five toes on hind foot, 1-3-1 grouping. Toes relatively slender. Claws short. Hind heel is haired and details are difficult to detect.

Trail: Bounding stride averages 7 inches (18 cm). Mostly terrestrial, it usually uses a half-bound, though full bounds may be observed in its trails.

Scat: Small, usually unconnected ovals.

scat
0.1 in diameter
0.3 cm

SCAT WIDTH

Habitat: Deciduous forest and brush areas.

Similar species: Smaller than ground and tree squirrels. Lacks the long claws of ground squirrel. Smaller than woochuck.

Other sign: Seeds and nuts of various plants, chewed open on one side.

front
0.5 x 0.4 in
1.3 x 1 cm

furred heel, not
included in track
measurement

hind
0.7 x 0.6 in
1.8 x 1.5 cm

bound

FRONT TRACK LENGTH

FRONT TRACK WIDTH

Eastern Gray Squirrel
Sciurus carolinensis

Large-sized squirrel, weighing up to 1.5 pounds (700 g). Grayish back with some brown in summer. Belly is whitish. Light colored ring around eye. Tail is bushy bordered with white hairs.

Track: Front foot size of a half dollar, with four toes in 1-2-1 grouping. Five toes on hind foot, 1-3-1 grouping. Toes relatively slender. Claws relatively short. Haired hind heel is indistinct in tracks.

Trail: Bounding stride ranges from 24 to 36 inches (60 to 90 cm). Straddle 5 inches (12.5 cm). Tends to use a full bound.

Scat: Small, shapeless black masses to small, usually unconnected ovals.

scat
0.25 in
0.6 cm

SCAT WIDTH

Habitat: Hardwood forests and river bottoms. Nut producing trees in territory.

Similar species: Larger than chipmunk. Lacks the long claws of ground squirrel. Larger than red squirrel and smaller than woodchuck.

Other sign: Nests in tree holes and builds twig-and-leaf nests in branches of trees, about 25 feet (7.6 m) from the ground.

hind
prints on
front

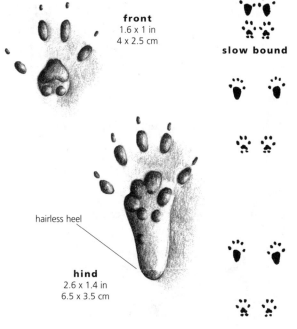

front
1.6 x 1 in
4 x 2.5 cm

slow bound

hairless heel

hind
2.6 x 1.4 in
6.5 x 3.5 cm

full bound

FRONT TRACK LENGTH

FRONT TRACK WIDTH

Southern Flying Squirrel
Glaucomys volans

A small squirrel, weighing 4
ounces (112 g). Its silky
fur is olive brown on
the back and lead gray
on the underside. A fold of skin
stretches between front and hind legs
and body, forming a wing and allowing
the squirrel to glide. Its bushy tail is
flattened to aid in sailing.

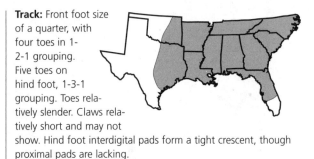

Track: Front foot size
of a quarter, with
four toes in 1-
2-1 grouping.
Five toes on
hind foot, 1-3-1
grouping. Toes rela-
tively slender. Claws relatively short and may not
show. Hind foot interdigital pads form a tight crescent, though
proximal pads are lacking.

Trail: Bounding stride averages 20 inches (50 cm). Uses a full
bound.

Scat: Small, usually unconnected ovals.

Habitat: Deciduous and coniferous forests, though often found
in attics of houses.

scat
0.1 in
0.3 cm

SCAT WIDTH

Similar species: Differs from all other squirrels and chipmunks by the tight crescent of interdigital pads on the hind foot. Lacks the long claws of ground squirrels. Smaller than woodchucks.

Other sign: Skin flap outlines may show in dust or snow. Sometimes builds roof on bird nest to use as den. Tree dens may hold 20 individuals during the winter.

hind prints on front

wing marks

front
0.5 x 0.5 in
1.3 x 1.3 cm

hind
1.5 x 0.5 in
3.8 x 1.3 cm

interdigital pads arrayed in a crescent shape

wing drag

bound

FRONT TRACK LENGTH

FRONT TRACK WIDTH

White-footed Mice

Peromyscus species

Small mouse, weighing up
to 1 ounce (28 g). Adult
white-footed mice (*P. leucopus*) are reddish brown to
brown on back with a white belly;
juveniles are dark gray on the back

White-footed mouse
Peromyscus leucopus

with a light gray belly. Large eyes and ears. Tail is long and
haired.

Track: Track smaller than a dime. Four toes on front foot, in 1-2-
1 grouping. Five toes
on hind foot, 1-3-1
grouping. Four
joined interdigi-
tal and two
proximal pads on
front footprint, five
joined pads and heel on
hind footprint. Heel is hairless.

Trail: Bounding stride of white-footed mice (illustrated here) averages 8 inches (20 cm). Species that use a full bound are climbers
and nest in grass, shrubs, or trees. Species using a half bound nest
on or below ground. Both types occasionally trot. Tail drag may be
present.

Scat: Oval-shaped pellets similar to those left by house mice.

scat
0.1 in
0.3 cm

SCAT WIDTH

Habitat: Ubiquitous, being found from deserts to the northern tree line, from below sea level to the top of high peaks.

Similar species: Differs from shrew by having only four toes on front feet and by being slightly larger. Differs from vole by often showing a tail drag and by most often bounding. Lacks the long heel of the jumping mouse. Smaller than chipmunk.

Other sign: Compact grass nests without entrances may be found under logs, rocks, and boards. Enters and exits through the grass wall, which closes up after passage. Caches large quantities of seeds in any convenient protected area. Leaves feces near and in nest.

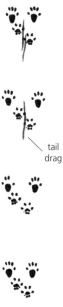

tail
drag

front
0.3 x 0.3 in
0.8 x 0.8 cm

remnant pad

4 x 4 bound

hind
0.4 x 0.3 in
1 x 0.8 cm

3 x 3 bound

FRONT TRACK LENGTH

FRONT TRACK WIDTH

Eastern Woodrat
Neotoma floridana

Size of a house rat, weighing about 10 to 16 ounces (280 to 450 g). Head gray, sides light brown; feet and belly are white. Densely haired long tail is white below and dark gray above. Back gray to reddish, belly and throat white to light gray. Large naked ears and long whiskers on face.

Track: Four toes with 1-2-1 spacing on front foot and five with a 1-3-1 on hind foot. Toes relatively slender, and toe pads slightly constricted. Three joined interdigital, one remnant, and two proximal pads in front footprint and three interdigital palm pads and two proximal pads on hind print.

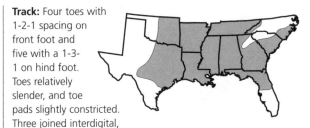

Trail: Bounding stride is 16 inches (40 cm) and walking stride is 6 inches (15 cm). Bounding is probably the most common gait, but woodrats also frequently walk.

Scat: Small oval pellets.

scat
0.2 in
0.4 cm

SCAT WIDTH

nest

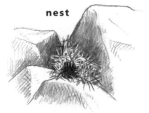

Habitat: Limestone caves, cliffs, talus slopes and residual sandstone boulders in beech, poplar, and maple forest. Uses abandoned buildings, especially outhouses.

Similar species: Larger than mice and voles. Differs from squirrels by the presence of heel pads on hind foot.

Other sign: Bulky houses may contain two or more nests. Houses are made from dry grass, shredded bark, fur, feathers, and twigs. Caches of food, including nuts, berries, foliage, and mushrooms, may be found on nest. Nearby post-office latrines on rocks may be used by several individuals, creating 2-inch (5-cm) deep masses of scat.

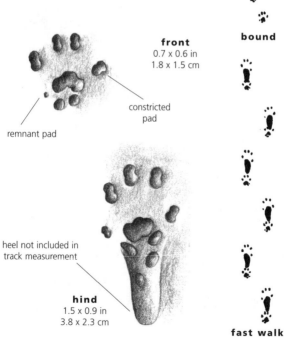

front
0.7 x 0.6 in
1.8 x 1.5 cm

constricted pad

remnant pad

heel not included in track measurement

hind
1.5 x 0.9 in
3.8 x 2.3 cm

bound

fast walk

FRONT TRACK LENGTH

FRONT TRACK WIDTH

Voles
Various species

Many species of mouse-sized mammals, related to lemmings and weighing up to 3 ounces (80 g). *Microtus pennsylvanicus* is gray to gray-brown on back, with a light colored belly. Small, stocky mammal with short ears and small eyes, almost hidden by fur. Short tail is sparsely haired. The more widely distributed, smaller, pine vole (*Pitymys pinetorum*) is auburn colored

Meadow vole
Microtus pennsylvanicus

Track: Track smaller than a dime. Four toes on front foot, in 1-2-1 grouping. Five toes on hind foot, 1-3-1 grouping. Four joined interdigital and two proximal pads on front footprint and four interdigital pads and one proximal on hind footprint. Heel is hairless.

Trail: Trotting stride 6 inches (15 cm). Usually trot, seldom bound. Tails usually do not show in the trail.

Scat: Oval-shaped pellets similar to those left by house mice; often piled in tennis ball–sized latrines, which may hold hundreds of pellets.

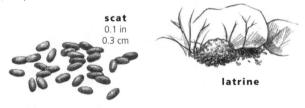

scat
0.1 in
0.3 cm

latrine

SCAT WIDTH

Habitat: *Microtus* species are grass-loving species, pine voles are most commonly found in deciduous forests.

Similar species: Differ from shrews by having only four toes on the front feet. Differ from mice by seldom showing a tail drag and by most often trotting. Lack the long heel of the jumping mouse. Pine vole tracks are smaller than *Microtus* vole tracks.

Other sign: As snow melts in spring, grass nests lacking entrances may be found. Snowmelt may also reveal 1-inch (2.5-cm) cords of grass and debris, stuffed into snow tunnels during the winter to make space elsewhere in the tunnel network. Vole latrines are usually found near nests, while mice leave feces near and in their nests. Worn runways through the grass.

bound

fast trot

trot

front
0.3 x 0.3 in
0.8 x 0.8 cm

heel not included in
track measurement

hind
0.4 x 0.3 in
1 x 0.8 cm

five pads
only

FRONT TRACK LENGTH

FRONT TRACK WIDTH

Meadow Jumping Mouse
Zapus hudsonius

A small mouse about 0.8 ounce (22 g) with long hind feet and long, sparsely haired tail. Yellowish sides, darker brown back, and white belly. White tip on long tail.

Track: Four toes on front foot, in 1-2-1 grouping. Hind foot is about the size of a quarter, exceptionally long and narrow, and has five toes in 1-3-1 grouping. Toes relatively slender. Heel is hairless.

Trail: Bounding stride 60 to 120 inches (150 to 300 cm). Makes sharp turns during travel. May cover considerable distance per stride when pursued. Tail drag often observed.

Scat: Small oval pellets.

scat
0.1 in
0.3 cm

SCAT WIDTH

Habitat: Riparian areas, seldom found more than 3 feet (1 m) from a stream. Occasionally meadows for feeding.

Similar species: Differs from other rodents in having long, narrow hind feet and tail drag. Differs from kangaroo rat by bounding from all four feet, not just hind.

Other sign: Small piles of grass stems left after eating. Round grass nests.

tail drag

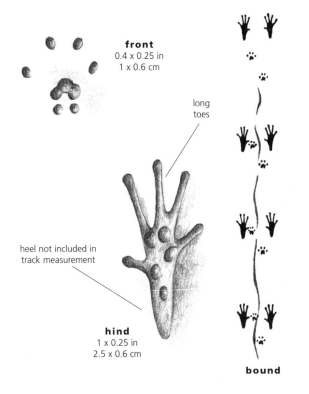

front
0.4 x 0.25 in
1 x 0.6 cm

long toes

heel not included in track measurement

hind
1 x 0.25 in
2.5 x 0.6 cm

bound

FRONT TRACK LENGTH

FRONT TRACK WIDTH

Muskrat
Ondatra zibethica

Large, ratlike, stocky, up to 4 pounds (2 kg). Males slightly larger than females. Small eyes and ears. Tail is black, flattened, scaly, with few hairs.

Track: Four toes on front foot (small fifth nubbin may show in very clear tracks) and five on hind foot. Toes very slender. Hind foot appears wider than long.

Trail: Walking strides averages 11 inches (28 cm). May lope with body turned to side.

Scat: Oval, at most three to four times longer than wide. Often deposited in a sticky mass on exposed logs at water's edge.

Habitat: Marshes and lake edges, secondarily on streambanks. Large rivers are not as frequently used. Cattails and rushes predominate.

scat
0.2 in
0.5 cm

SCAT WIDTH

Similar species: Differs from beaver by smaller size and lack of webbing. Differs from mink by long, slender toes and by usually walking.

Other sign: Small conical domes made from reeds serve as dens. Cut grass and reeds near water's edge mark feeding sites. Muskrats make "post offices," repeated scat deposits, on rocks.

4 x 4 bound

3 x 3 bound

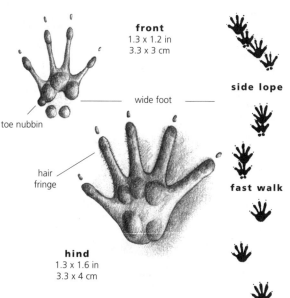

post office

front
1.3 x 1.2 in
3.3 x 3 cm

wide foot

toe nubbin

hair fringe

side lope

fast walk

walk

hind
1.3 x 1.6 in
3.3 x 4 cm

FRONT TRACK LENGTH

FRONT TRACK WIDTH

Beaver
Castor canadensis

Largest rodent in North America, 30 to 60 pounds (14 to 27 kg). Distinguished by large, webbed hind feet and large, horizontally flattened tail. Fur overall is dark brown to almost black, with lighter belly.

Track: Front and hind prints show five toes. Hind foot may be larger than a human hand. Webbing between hind toes shows, but only when pulled tight by splaying of toes. Clear tracks are difficult to find, as the hind foot steps on the front foot and the dragging tail obliterates many prints.

Trail: Walking stride 18 inches (45 cm).

Scat: Seldom found; usually deposited in water, where they disintegrate quickly. Marshmallow-sized, a little longer than thick. Consist of wood chips.

Habitat: Seldom found far from a creek, river, pond, or lake.

scat
1 x 0.7 in
2.5 x 1.8 cm

SCAT WIDTH

Similar species: Differs from other rodents by large size and webbing. Differs from river otter by long, slender toes and pointed heel, and by lacking a chevron-shaped pad.

Other sign: Dams and conical lodges, built of twigs and sticks. Standing, cutoff tree trunks end in a tapered cone. Debarked tree limbs in the water.

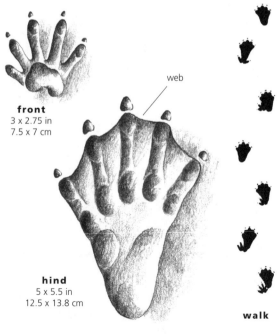

lodge

front
3 x 2.75 in
7.5 x 7 cm

web

hind
5 x 5.5 in
12.5 x 13.8 cm

walk

FRONT TRACK LENGTH

FRONT TRACK WIDTH

Porcupine
Erethizon dorsatum

Basketball-sized or
large, 10 to 25 pounds
(5 to 11 kg). Stocky
body, with short legs.
Distinguished by the
presence of quills. Brown
to yellowish-brown in color.

Track: Rough texture formed by small nubs on soles of feet. Four toes on front foot and five toes on hind. Toes often do not show. Claws often show.

Trail: Walking stride 17 inches (43 cm). Tail drag often present.

Scat: Winter scat formed from feeding on conifers is red. Summer scat includes more herbs and shrubs and is brown to black. Scat from both seasons may be composed of individual pellets or strings of pellets connected by fibers.

scat
0.5 in
1.3 cm

**debarked
stick
with
chew
marks**

SCAT WIDTH

Habitat: Generally found near forests, but may be far from trees if shrubs are available.

Similar species: Rough texture on sole of foot is diagnostic. In snow, trough made by dragging belly highlights its stockiness, separating it from faster-moving mammals.

Other sign: Twigs with bark chewed off, found at bases of trees. Will perch in a tree for days chewing the bark, thereby killing the tree.

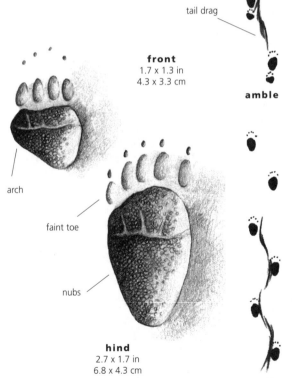

tail drag

front
1.7 x 1.3 in
4.3 x 3.3 cm

amble

arch

faint toe

nubs

hind
2.7 x 1.7 in
6.8 x 4.3 cm

walk

FRONT TRACK LENGTH

FRONT TRACK WIDTH

Nutria

Myocastor coypus

Muskratlike rodent weighing 15 to 20 pounds (6.8 to 9 kg). Gray to brown with long, nearly naked round tail. Introduced from South America for fur farming. Escapes are widely distributed.

Track: Four toes on front foot (small fifth nubbin may show in very clear tracks) and five on hind foot. Front print with three interdigital and two proximal pads. Hind print with five interdigital pads and joined proximal pads. Hind foot webbed except between toes 4 and 5.
Detached claws.

Trail: Walking stride 12 to 14 inches (30 to 36 cm). Occasionally gallops with one measured stride of 18 inches (45 cm).
Walking straddle is 4 to 7 inches (10 to 18 cm).

Scat: We have not recorded their scat.

Habitat: Wetlands, including marshes, swamps, and lakes.

Similar species: Four toes on front and five toes on hind print identify as a rodent. Large size and webbing separate it from most other rodents. Lack of webbing between toes 4 and 5 separates it from beaver.

Other sign: Burrows in banks with entrances above water. Nest built in shallow-water vegetation.

amble

front
2.1 x 1.6 in
5.3 x 4 cm

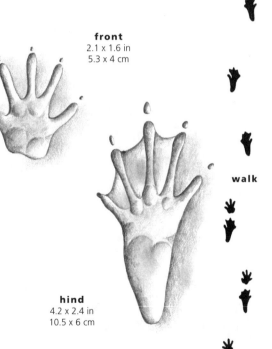

walk

hind
4.2 x 2.4 in
10.5 x 6 cm

slow walk

FRONT TRACK LENGTH

FRONT TRACK WIDTH

White-tailed Deer
Odocoileus virginianus

Smallest member of the deer family. Male averages 130 pounds (60 kg), female about 110 pounds (50 kg). Coat is reddish in summer and blue-gray in winter. The prominent white tail is carried erect when animal disturbed. Antlers, found only on male, have tines, or points, branching off main beam.

Track: Heart shaped, with convex wall. Pad occupies most of the clout; subunguinis slender.

Trail: Walking stride 30 inches (75 cm). Pronks or stots with front and hind feet striking the ground at the same time. Gallops when in a hurry.

Scat: Usually dry, falls apart when it hits the ground. Pellets vary from nipple-dimple shape to oval.

scat
pellet 0.3 in
pellet 0.8 cm

antler

SCAT WIDTH

Habitat: Generally closed timber, but moves out to grasslands at twilight to feed.

Similar species: Differs from boar by their pointed clouts, narrower splay, and closely spaced dewclaws.

Other sign: Breaks off limbs of trees when removing velvet from antlers. Velvet is difficult to find, as both deer and rodents eat the nutrient-rich material. Height of tree wound indicates animal height.

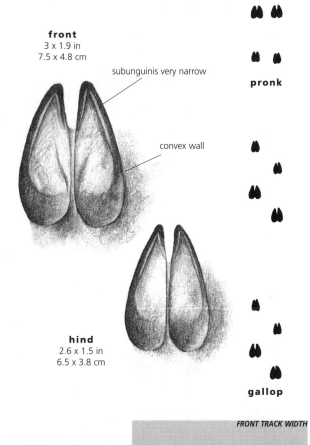

front
3 x 1.9 in
7.5 x 4.8 cm

subunguinis very narrow

convex wall

pronk

hind
2.6 x 1.5 in
6.5 x 3.8 cm

gallop

FRONT TRACK LENGTH

FRONT TRACK WIDTH

Wild Boar / Feral Hog
Sus species

Medium to large-sized
pig, weights to more
than 220 pounds (100
kg). Boars show
great variability as
they may be a mixture
of European wild boars, recent
domestic hogs, and feral hogs.
Colors may be black; black and brown; or white, brown, and
roan. Hair is coarse and dense. States below indicated with a
(B) have many widely scattered occurances of boars.

Track: Deer-sized
tracks. Clouts
are rounded
and blunt at
the tip. Hooves
tend to splay.
Dewclaws are more
pointed and register up
to 0.5 inch (1.3 cm) outside
and up to 2 inches (5 cm) behind the hooves.

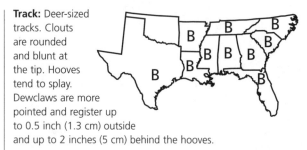

Trail: Walking stride is 25 inches (65 cm). Trotting stride is about
55 inches (140 cm).

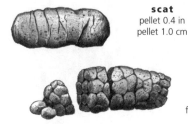

soft

scat
pellet 0.4 in
pellet 1.0 cm

firm

SCAT WIDTH

Scat: Seasonally varies from formless on wet, spring diet to pellets to clumps of pellets on dry diets. Diameter of clumps of pellets may be over 2 inches (5 cm).

Habitat: Scattered distribution in swamps, marshes, and bottomland with mixed deciduous forests. Dense understory and moist soft soil are preferred. Raised dry areas for nests.

Similar species: Differs from deer by their blunt, rounded clouts, greater splay, and widely spaced dewclaws.

Other sign: Boars root up the earth and wallow. Trees are rubbed to 36 inches (90 cm). Nests are shallow depressions in dry ground, occasionally lined with vegetation.

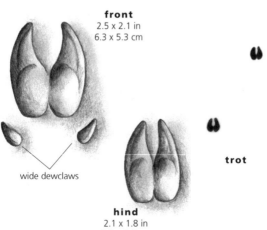

walk

front
2.5 x 2.1 in
6.3 x 5.3 cm

wide dewclaws

hind
2.1 x 1.8 in
5.3 x 4.5 cm

trot

Selected reading

Tracks and tracking

Bang, P., et al. 1972. *Collins Guide to Animal Tracks and Signs*. London: Collins Sons.

Brown, R., J. Ferguson, M. Lawrence, and D. Lees. 1987. *Tracks and Signs of the Birds of Britain and Europe: An Identification Guide*. Kent, England: Christopher Helm.

Brunner, J. 1909. *Tracks and Tracking*. New York: Outing.

Fjelline, D. P. and T. M. Mansfield. 1989. "Method to standardize the procedure for measuring mountain lion tracks." In *Proceedings of the Third Mountain Lion Workshop*, ed. R. H. Smith, 49–51. Prescott, Arizona: Arizona Game and Fish Department.

Forrest, L. R. 1988. *Field Guide to Tracking Animals in Snow*. Harrisburg, Pennsylvania: Stackpole Books.

Halfpenny, J. C. 1997. *Tracking: Mastering the Basics*. 180 min. A Naturalist's World. Videocassette.

—1986a. *A Field Guide to Mammal Tracking in North America*. Boulder, Colorado: Johnson.

—1986b. *Tracks and Tracking: A "How To" Guide*. Gardiner, Montana: A Naturalist's World. Slides.

Halfpenny, J. C., et al. 1996. "Snow tracking." In *American Marten, Fisher, Lynx, and Wolverines: Survey Methods for Their Detection*, ed. W. Zielinski and T. Kucera, 91–163. General Technical Report PSW-GTR-157. Berkeley, California: USDA Forest Service, Pacific Southwest Research Station.

Headstrom, R. 1971. *Identifying Animals Tracks: Mammals, Birds, and Other Animals of the Eastern United States*. New York: Dover.

Murie, O. 1954. *A Field Guide to Animal Tracks*. Peterson Field Guide Series, no. 9. Boston: Houghton Mifflin.

Rezendes, P. 1999. *Tracking and the Art of Seeing: How to Read Animal Tracks and Sign*. 2nd Ed. Charlotte, Vermont: Camden House.

Seton, E. T. 1958. *Animal Tracks and Hunter Signs*. New York: Doubleday.

Recommended field identification guides

Burt, W. H. and R. P. Grossenheider. 1964. *A Field Guide to the Mammals*. Peterson Field Guide Series, no. 5. Boston: Houghton Mifflin.

Chandlers, S. R., B. Bruun, and H. S. Zim. 1983. *A Guide to Field Identification: Birds of North America*. New York: Golden.

Conant, R. 1958. *Reptiles and Amphibians of Eastern and Central North America*. Peterson Field Guide Series, no. 12. Boston: Houghton Mifflin.

Gosner, K. L. 1985. *Atlantic Seashore*. Norwalk, Connecticut: The Easton Press.

National Geographic Society. 1983. *Field Guide to the Birds of North America*. Washington, D.C.: National Geographic Society.

Peterson, R. T. 1984. *Birds of the Eastern United States*. Norwalk, Connecticut: The Easton Press.

Index

About the authors

JAMES HALFPENNY has searched for dinosaur tracks in Colorado and Montana, tracked wildlife in Tanzania and Kenya, studied endangered species on China's Tibet-Qinghai plateau, and researched the polar bears of Hudson Bay and Greenland. Jim is a member of the International Society of Professional Trackers. Since 1961 he has taught outdoor and environmental education for a vast array of schools and organizations, including the Smithsonian, National Outdoor Leadership School, Outward Bound, the Appalachian Mountain Club, The Wilderness Society, National Wildlife Federation, Defenders of Wildlife, and the National Audubon Society. He has trained rangers in tracking techniques at Yellowstone, Glacier, Grand Teton, and Rocky Mountain national parks. His research has also taken him to Antarctica and all over North America. Halfpenny has been featured, with Australian aborigines, Kalahari Bushmen, and Alaskan Inuits, in a documentary about the loss of native tracking skills shown on the Discovery Channel. He is a past field director and project coordinator for the University of Colorado's Institute of Arctic and Alpine Research. He is also the senior author of the *Scats and Tracks* series, *A Field Guide to Mammal Tracking in North America*, *Discovering Yellowstone Wolves: Watcher's Guide*, and *Winter: an Ecological Handbook*. He lives just outside Yellowstone National Park in Gardiner, Montana.

JIM BRUCHAC, a descendant of Slavic and Abenaki Indian woodsmen, was born and raised in the foothills of the Adirondacks. Jim is a professional storyteller, author, and licensed New York State Wilderness Guide. Jim's first interest in animal tracking came from his father, Dr.

Joseph Bruchac III, coauthor of the *Keepers of The Earth* series. Other influences include his late grandfather, Joseph Bruchac, Jr., The Adirondack Taxidermist, noted outdoorsman and member of the Taxidermy Hall of Fame, as well as Jim's continued work with John Stokes, founder of the Tracking Project. Since his first introductions to James Halfpenny in 1996, the two have spent over a hundred hours tracking together out West. Jim is a member of the International Society of Professional Trackers. Over the years Jim has offered numerous animal tracking programs for schools and organizations, including The National Wildlife Federation, New York State Parks, Cornell Outdoor Education, The National Park Service, The Nature Conservancy, and The Environmental Education Council of Ohio. Jim's past publications include *Scats and Tracks of the Northeast* (Falcon), *When The Chenoo Howls, Native Tales of Terror* (Walker Books), *Native American Games and Stories* (Fulcrum Publishing), *How Chipmunk Got Its Stripes* (Dial Books), and *At Home on the Earth* (Modern Curriculum Press). He lives in Greenfield Center, New York.

About the illustrator

TODD TELANDER is a freelance natural science illustrator and wildlife artist. He studied biology and environmental studies at the University of California, Santa Cruz, where he became interested in illustration. His work appears in Falcon's *America's 100 Most Wanted Birds*, *Birder's Dictionary*, *A Field Guide to Cows*, and *A Field Guide to Pigs* as well as in museums, galleries, and private collections. Todd lives in New Mexico.